Instructor's Manual with Test Item File

Allen B. Asch
Laurie S. Chin

Hospitality Cost Control
A Practical Approach

Allen B. Asch

Upper Saddle River, New Jersey 07458

Pearson Education LTD.
Pearson Education Singapore, Pte. Ltd.
Pearson Education Canada, Ltd.
Pearson Education–Japan
Pearson Education Australia PTY, Limited
Pearson Education North Asia Ltd.
Pearson Educación de Mexico, S.A. de C.V.
Pearson Education Malaysia, Pte. Ltd.

10 9 8 7 6 5 4 3 2 1
ISBN 0-13-111602-9

Contents

Preface

This manual is designed to assist instructors in using *Hospitality Cost Control* to teach food and beverage cost control to culinary and hospitality majors. This manual includes a course outline, scheduling tips, chapter objectives, and a test bank for each chapter. The answers to the textbook problems, as well as to the accompanying student workbook problems (Student Workbook ISBN 0-13-174768-1), are included. Some workbook problem answers are omitted if they are subjective.

Suggested Course Syllabus

INSTRUCTOR:

PHONE:

FAX:

E-MAIL:

OFFICE HOURS:

WEB SITE:

TEACHING PHILOSOPHY

As an outcome-based educator, my main objective is for you to learn the material presented. Keeping this in mind, certain material will be asked on subsequent tests.

COURSE DESCRIPTION

This course will explain the duties and responsibilities of the manager for budgeting, forecasting, costs, and developing and maintaining internal controls in all types of food and beverage operations.

Prerequisites

There are four major topics:

1. Food cost control
2. Beverage cost control
3. Labor cost control
4. Other controllable expenses

COURSE OBJECTIVES

By the end of this course, you will be able to:

1. prepare and analyze operating budgets.
2. calculate standard and actual costs.
3. analyze operating costs and operating cost percentages.
4. perform profit and loss statement calculations.
5. analyze the relationships between sales, expenses, and profits.
6. recognize control deficiencies and institute corrective actions.

REQUIRED TEXTBOOK

Hospitality Cost Control: A Practical Approach, First Edition, by Allen B. Asch.

COURSE REQUIREMENTS

To attain the objectives of this course, we will rely primarily on readings, lectures, discussions, quizzes, and tests.

There will be five tests, including the final exam, given throughout the semester. Unless prior arrangements have been made, missed tests cannot be made up once they are returned and reviewed in class. There will be a few take-home quizzes and unannounced in-class quizzes during the semester.

ASSIGNMENT/TEST BREAKDOWN

Tests (four)	400 points
Final exam	100 points
Excel assignment (pass/fail)	50 points
Pop quiz/classroom assignments/homework	50 points
Total points	600 points

TESTS

There will be five tests, each worth 100 points. The tests will be a combination of multiple choice, true/false, fill-in-the-blank, short answer, and mathematical problems. Please bring a Scantron Sheet and a calculator to each exam. There may be occasional pop quizzes in class. There will also be homework and in-class assignments.

EXCEL ASSIGNMENT

There will be an assignment utilizing Microsoft® Excel in which you will be required to write a program (including formulas) that will simulate the extended math problems we will be talking about in class. This assignment is pass/fail, but the assignment may be handed in early to ensure it is correct.

(Suggestions may include a butcher's yield/cooking loss program, or an operating budget assignment with changes as the period goes on.)

POP QUIZ/HOMEWORK

There will be five graded in-class assignments or homework collections for 10 points each. The homework and any in-class assignments will be relevant to class material and many will be used to reinforce material covered in class.

GRADING SCALE

The total number of points earned for assignments and tests will be divided by the total maximum number of points available. This percentage will then be converted into a letter grade according to the following scale.

A	=	93%–100%	A-	=	90%–92%
B+	=	87%–89%	B	=	83%–86%
B-	=	80%–82%	C+	=	77%–79%
C	=	73%–76%	C-	=	70%–73%
D	=	60%–69%	F	=	Below 60%

ATTENDANCE AND PARTICIPATION

Good attendance and participation mean being present, on time, courteous, informed, awake, and attentive. Good attendance and participation are expected. Sign-in attendance sheets will be circulated daily in class. Excused absences can be authorized providing that the request is reasonable, not work related, and documented in writing.

Whether or not in attendance, you are responsible for material from all class meetings, including lecture notes, handouts, assignments, due dates, and being aware of schedule changes.

ACADEMIC INTEGRITY

You are expected, at all times, to perform your own work. Acts of academic misconduct include, but are not limited to, plagiarism, cheating on exams, signing another student's name on an attendance sheet, or any other deceptive activity associated with class points.

Points Earned

Test one	________	(100)
Test two	________	(100)
Test three	________	(100)
Test four	________	(100)
Final exam	________	(100)
Excel assignment	________	(50)
Pop quiz/class assignment or homework	________	(10)
Pop quiz/class assignment or homework	________	(10)
Pop quiz/class assignment or homework	________	(10)
Pop quiz/class assignment or homework	________	(10)
Pop quiz/class assignment or homework	________	(10)
Total points	________	600 points

SUGGESTED COURSE SCHEDULE

Class 1	Introduction, Chapter 1, Quiz 1
Class 2	Chapters 1 and 2
Class 3	Chapters 2 and 3
Class 4	Chapter 4
Class 5	Chapter 4
Class 6	Chapter 4
Class 7	Chapter 4, Quiz 2
Class 8	Chapter 4
Class 9	Test 1
Class 10	Chapter 5
Class 11	Chapter 6
Class 12	Chapter 6
Class 13	Chapter 7
Class 14	Chapter 7, Quiz 3
Class 15	Chapter 7
Class 16	Test 2
Class 17	Chapter 8
Class 18	Chapter 9
Class 19	Test 3
Class 20	Chapter 10
Class 21	Chapter 11
Class 22	Test 4
Class 23	Chapter 12
Class 24	Chapter 13
Class 25	Chapter 14, Excel assignment due
Class 26	Chapter 15
Class 27	FINAL EXAM

1

Introduction

CHAPTER OBJECTIVES

After finishing this chapter the students will be able to:

- Describe reasons restaurants fail
- Differentiate among statistical data in the hospitality industry
- Relate management's role in cost control
- Define the control process
- Distinguish between basic cost control terminologies
- Differentiate between fixed costs and variable costs
- Differentiate between controllable costs and non-controllable costs
- Examine the concept of total sales
- Calculate sales mix
- Differentiate between basic cost control formulas

ANSWERS TO TEXT PROBLEMS

1. Answers will vary. rent, insurance, window washing, salaried employees, depreciation
2. Answers will vary. food + beverage costs, labor costs,
3. Item A—20.64% Item B—27.91% Item C—6.30%
   Item D—7.91% Item E—15.11% Item F—22.12%
4. $7,139.07
5. $16,590.37
6. 27.85%
7. $9,841.01
8. 26.85%
9. $5,436.13
10. $4,841.47
11. 23.95%
12. 24.43%
13. $183.52
14. $48.45
15. $35,509.89
16. $1,840.85
17. 18.99%
18. $74,914.21

19. 26.18%
20. $10,627.49
21. $5.52
22. $349.42
23. $162,406.91
24. Item A—10.6% Item B—12.03% Item C—17.48%
    Item D—18.91% Item E—30.95% Item F—10.03%
25. $6,538.27
26. $11,124.91
27. Writing off of expenses of a commercial building over a period of 15 years.
28. Can deduct the amount from profits, thus lowering taxes.

ANSWERS TO WORKBOOK PROBLEMS

1. a. $5
   b. $2.50
   c. $1
   What do these numbers mean to you? See page 21 text.
2. a. Average food cost: $5
   b. Average labor cost: $2.50
   c. Total average cost: $8.50
   d. Average sales: $20.00
3. a. steaks: 20 33%
   b. seafood: 19 31.60%
   c. poultry: 15 25%
   d. vegetarian: 6 10%
4. a. Food cost %: 33.33%
   b. Labor cost %: 13.30%

5. Fill in the blank cells in the following table:

Number of customers	Sales	Food cost	Food cost %	Beverage cost	Beverage cost %	Labor cost	Labor cost %	Average sales/ person
200	$1,000	**$200**	20	**$100**	10	**$400**	40	**$5.00**
750	$2,000	**$400**	20	**$400**	20	**$800**	40	**$2.67**
1,000	$3,000	**$1,050**	35	**$900**	30	**$600**	20	**$3.00**
2,000	$4,000	**$1,600**	40	**$1,600**	40	**$800**	20	**$2.00**
200	**$1,000**	$300	**33.3**	$200	**20**	$200	**20**	$5.00
750	**$4,500**	$2,000	**44.4**	$1,000	**22.2**	$1,000	**22.2**	$6.00
1,000	**$7,000**	$2,000	**28.6**	$1,000	**14.3**	$2,000	**28.3**	$7.00
2,000	**$16,000**	$6,000	**37.5**	$1,000	**6.3**	$2,000	**12.5**	$8.00

6. a. Labor cost %: 21.3
   b. The amount spent on food: $4,500
7. a. Labor cost: $3,200
   b. Food cost: $7,500
   c. Food cost %: 30
8.

Total sales	Number of customers	Fixed cost per customer
$5,000	1,000	**$5.00**
$10,000	2,000	**$2.50**
$15,000	3,000	**$1.67**
$20,000	4,000	**$1.25**

9. a. FC = $250
      FC % = 25
   b. FC = 1,000
      FC % = 33.33
   c. a. $600
      b. $1,200
      c. 33.33

10.

	Brian's Restaurant		Tina's Restaurant	
Revenue	$1,000,000	XXXXXX	$1,000,000	XXXXXX
Variable Costs	$500,000	50%	$300,000	30%
Fixed Costs	$400,000	40%	$600,000	60%
Total Costs	**$900,000**	XXXXXX	**$900,000**	XXXXXX
Profit	**$100,000**	**10%**	**$100,000**	**10%**

Both restaurants are equal.

	Brian's Restaurant		Tina's Restaurant	
Revenue	**$1,000,000**	XXXXXX	**$1,200,000**	XXXXXX
Variable Costs	**$500,000**	50%	**$360,000**	30%
Fixed Costs	$400,000	**33.3%**	$600,000	**50%**
Total Costs	**$1,000,000**	XXXXXX	**$960,000**	XXXXXX
Profit	**$200,000**	**16.6%**	**$240,000**	**20%**

What restaurant would now be the best? Why did this happen? Tina's

2

An Overview of Cost Control

CHAPTER OBJECTIVES

After finishing this chapter the students will be able to:

- Differentiate among the three standards used in food and beverage: quality, quantity, and cost
- Calculate food cost using the basic formula for food cost
- Differentiate between asset and debit calculations for food cost
- Calculate food cost percent
- Utilize an operating budget
- Perform a make or buy analysis
- Investigate outsourcing
- Recognize techniques of revenue control
- Discriminate among the various threats to profit due to theft

ANSWERS TO TEXT PROBLEMS

1. Quality standard is a standard determined by management regarding ingredients, plates, decorations, and many other facets of the establishment. Should prime grade beef be served, or is choice the acceptable quality? Should silver be the standard for silverware, or does stainless steel fit the client profile?
2. Quantity standard is a standard determined by management regarding food, labor, and supplies. How much food should be served? Should five shrimp or eight shrimp be the quantity standard? Should a 60-count or an 80-count potato be served with entrees? Should there be front and back waiters, or just one waiter per table?
3. Price/cost standard is associated with the raw costs of items, as well as the menu price. Should food cost percent be an overall 25% of menu price or be closer to 27%?

4.

Food Sales						
	Average check	Turnover	Seats	Days	Weeks	
Lunch						
Weekdays	$4.43	1.7	120	5	52	$234,967.20
Dinner 885,880.30						
Weekdays	$8.31	2.0	120	4	52	$414,835.20
Fri/Sat	$11.56	2.4	120	2	52	$346,245.12
Sunday	$10.00	2.0	120	1	52	$124,800.00
Total						$1,120,847.52
Beverage Sales						
Lunch						$35,245.08
Dinner						$177,176.06
Total						$212,421.14
Total Sales						$1,333,268.66
Food Cost						$313,837.31
Beverage Cost						$38,235.81
Total Cost						$352,073.11
Salaries						$133,326.87
Wages						$266,653.73
Employee Benefits						$71,996.51
Other Controllable Expense						$66,663.43
Occupancy Cost						$27,345.00
Interest						$9,453.00
Depreciation						$10,000.00
Profit/loss						$395,757.01

5.

Food Sales						
	Average Check	Turnover	Seats	Days	Weeks	
Lunch						
Weekdays	$4.43	1.7	120	5	52	$234,967.20
Dinner						
Weekdays	$8.31	2.0	120	4	52	$414,835.20
Fri/Sat	$11.56	2.4	120	2	52	$346,245.12
Sunday	$10.00	2.0	120	1	52	$124,800.00
Total						$1,120,847.52
Beverage Sales						
Lunch						$35,245.08
Dinner						$177,176.06
Total						$212,421.14
Total Sales						$1,333,268.66
Food Cost						$336,254.26
Beverage Cost						$42,484.23
Total Cost						$378,738.48
Salaries						$146,659.55
Wages						$266,653.73
Employee Benefits						$74,396.39
Other Controllable Expense						$59,997.09
Occupancy Cost						$27,345.00
Interest						$9,453.00
Depreciation						$10,000.00
Profit/loss						$360,025.41

6. | Item | Cost |
   |---|---|
   | Water | Free |
   | Yeast | \$0.75 |
   | Flour | \$2.24 |
   | Salt | \$0.15 |
   | Malt syrup | \$0.06 |
   | Sugar | \$0.03 |
   | Shortening | \$0.08 |

   It is more cost effective to make them for \$0.33 each.
7. \$29,203
8. 27.4%
9. 19.23%
10. 9475 + 42155 – 11475 – 34 + 816 + 140 – 280 – 751 – 267 – 1280.02 (4621 × .277) = \$38,498.98
11. | Item | Cost |
    |---|---|
    | Shortening | \$0.23 |
    | Sugar | \$0.24 |
    | Vanilla | \$0.38 |
    | Eggs | \$0.30 |
    | Cocoa | \$1.20 |
    | Flour | \$0.81 |
    | Buttermilk | \$1.59 |
    | Labor | \$0.54 |

    Make the cakes for \$5.29.

12.

Food Sales						
	Average Check	Turnover	Seats	Days	Weeks	
Lunch						
Weekdays	$6.20	1.3	210	5	52	$440,076.00
Weekend	$7.00	1.3	210	1	52	$99,372.00
Dinner						
Weekdays	$9.75	1.4	210	4	52	$596,232.00
Fri/Sat	$12.00	1.8	210	2	52	$471,744.00
Sunday	$10.54	1.4	210	1	52	$161,135.52
Total						$1,768,559.52
Beverage Sales						
Lunch						$64,733.76
Dinner						$233,531.19
Total						$298,264.95
Total Sales						$2,066,824.47
Food Cost						$583,624.64
Beverage Cost						$59,652.99
Total Cost						$643,277.63
Salaries						$289,355.43
Wages						$268,687.18
Employee Benefits						$84,739.80
Other Controllable Expense						$124,009.47
Occupancy Cost						$83,000.00
Interest						$16,500.00
Depreciation						$58,000.00
Profit/loss						$499,254.96

13.

Food Sales						
	Average Check	Turnover	Seats	Days	Weeks	
Lunch						
Weekdays	$5.50	1.3	210	5	52	$390,390.00
Weekend	$7.00	1.3	210	1	52	$99,372.00
Dinner						
Weekdays	$9.75	1.4	210	4	52	$596,232.00
Fri/Sat	$12.00	1.8	210	2	52	$471,744.00
Sunday	$10.54	1.4	210	1	52	$161,135.52
Total						$1,718,873.52
Beverage Sales						
Lunch						$58,771.44
Dinner						$233,531.19
Total						$292,302.63
Total Sales						$2,011,176.15
Food Cost						$550,039.53
Beverage Cost						$58,460.53
Total Cost						$608,500.05
Salaries						$261,452.90
Wages						$261,452.90
Employee Benefits						$78,435.87
Other Controllable Expense						$140,782.33
Occupancy Cost						$83,000.00
Interest						$16,500.00
Depreciation						$58,000.00
Profit/loss						$503,052.10

ANSWERS TO WORKBOOK PROBLEMS

1. Food, beverage, labor
2. OI – EI + P = CF
3. CF = $1,100
4. CF = $1,100
5. CF = $1,100 – 30 = $1,070
6. CF = $1,020
7. CF % = CF / sales
8. a. FC% = 50%
   b. FC% = 33.33%
   c. FC% = 16.67%
   d. FC% = 22.50%
9. CF = $937.50 Benefits = $375.00
10. $1,875
11. $1,200
12. $2,400
13. $14,400
14. Premade cost less by $15.00
15. a. Food cost = $1,400
    b. FC% = 29.20%
16. a. Total Sales: $1,800
    b. CF: $400
    c. CF%: 22.20%
    d. Profit: $1,400
17. CF = $250; CF% = 41.7%
18. $CF = \frac{\$1,300}{\$3,800}$; CF% = 34.2%

3

Controlling Costs and Improving Revenue Control with Technology

CHAPTER OBJECTIVES

After finishing this chapter the students will be able to:

- Analyze why technology is created
- Analyze technology for the hospitality industry
- Evaluate technology available for the guest
- Evaluate computer technology used for purchasing and warehousing
- Evaluate technology in the processes of production, sales increases, and revenue control
- Examine advances in product packaging
- Evaluate the value of Point of Sale equipment
- Evaluate negative responses to technology

ANSWERS TO TEXT PROBLEMS

1. Guest driven, cost control, generate increased sales and control revenue, and labor cost savings.
2. The main cause is the lack of money for small companies. Therefore, only large companies are buying new technology.
3. The major impact is loss of entry-level jobs to new machines and equipment. Lost jobs may include front desk workers, PBX operators, or travel agents.
4. The development of ovens that cook using both dry and moist heat. Additionally, menu planning technology and convenience foods have grown.
5. Answers will vary but may include POS system for ordering and inventory control, savings in cooking time or cost, customer satisfaction.
6. Sous vide, modified atmosphere packing, and ultra high temp pasteurization.
7. Point of sale equipment allows charges to be posted to the correct ledger. It may control quality and warn when shelf life is coming to an end.
8. Answers will vary, but may include robotics or certain wireless technologies.
9. Data mining allows users to find hidden details about customers in the database, allowing for better customer service.
10. Smart cards allow hotel guest to purchase mini bar products, dinners, and retail items using their room key. This allows for more convenience for the guest.

11. Fingerprint technology will drive the future of technology.
12. Answers will vary but may include these.
    Customer satisfaction: Data mining for guest room ambience and smart cards
    Decrease in labor: Self-ordering kiosks and robotic cooking
    Efficiency of operations: Unique packaging and recipe conversion
13. Answers depend on the perspective of the individual.
14. Answers will vary.

ANSWERS TO WORKBOOK DISCUSSION QUESTIONS

3. Point of sale upgrades
4. Computerized ordering
5. Record sales, changes in sales, record individual items sold

4

Cost–Volume–Profit Relationships

CHAPTER OBJECTIVES

After finishing this chapter the students will be able to:

- Explain variable costs
- Describe the variable rate
- Describe the components of the contribution margin
- Describe the contribution margin
- Calculate the variable cost and rate, contribution margin and rate, and calculate the break-even point in sales dollars and sales units
- Determine which formula to use for various calculations

ANSWERS TO TEXT PROBLEMS

Different formulas may be used to calculate the correct answers in the following problems.

1. a. s – fc – p = vc
      vc = $6,357
   b. s × vr = vc
      vc = $40,131.98
   c. s – cm = vc
      vc = $4.53
   d. s × cr = cm
      cm = $15,396.08
      s – cm = vc
      vc = $12,096.92
   e. cm / cr = s
      s = $310,586.89
      s – cm = vc
      vc = $121,128.89

2. a. s – vc – p = fc
   fc = $9,144
   b. s × vr = vc
   vc = $123,393.60
   s – vc + loss = fc
   fc = $230,928.40
   c. cm – p = fc
   fc = $143,880
3. a. s – vc = cm
   cm = $8.03
   b. s × vr = vc
   vc = $40,450.41
   s – vc = cm
   cm = $82,126.59
   c. s × cr = cm
   cm = $333,875.10
4. a. fc + p + cm = s
   s = $45,993
   b. vc / vr = s
   s = $34.10
   c. vc / vr = s
   s = $162,739.29
   d. cm / cr = s
   s = $90,254.69
   e. cm + vc = s
   s = $21,207
   f. cm / cr = s
   s = $14.54
5. a. (fc + p) / cm = s
   s = $8,964
   b. (fc + p) / cm = s
   s = $844
   c. (fc + p) / cm = s
   s = $32,881
6. a. vc / s = vr
   vr = 36.78%
   b. vc / s = vr
   vr = 39.85%
   c. vc / s = vr
   vr = 50.90%

7. a. vc / s = vr
   vr = 57.45%
   b. vc / s = vr
   vr = 68.64%
   c. vc / s = vr
   vr = 65.46%
8. a. s – fc – vc = p
   p = $25,359.48
   b. s – fc – vc = p
   p = $2.77
   c. s – fc – vc = p
   p = $1,236.74
9. a. (fc + p) / cr = bes
   bes = $8,4541.82
   b. (fc + p) / cr = bes
   bes = $265,738.81
   c. (fc + p) / cr = bes
   bes = $75,063.93
10. a. (fc + p) / cm = beu
   beu = 7,419
   b. (fc + p) / cm = beu
   beu = 5,150
   c. (fc + p) / cm = beu
   beu = 31,699
11. Change the quality, quantity, or cost standard.
12. The fixed cost and the profit generated by sales.
13. Percentage of sales that goes toward the variable costs.
14. Percentage of sales that goes toward the contribution margin.
15. It determines the amount of sales needed to make the business self-sufficient.
16.

Item	**Cost/Selling Price**	**Number Sold**	**Total Cost**	**Total Sales**
Steak	$7.75/$17.95	15	$116.25	$269.25
Chicken	$4.79/$13.95	26	$124.54	$362.70
Fish	$3.99/$12.95	11	$43.89	$142.45
Duck	$6.57/$16.95	8	$52.56	$135.60
Total		60	$337.24	$910.00
	Average contribution margin: $9.55	Average variable rate: 37.06%	Average variable cost: $5.62	Average check: $15.17

17.

Item	Cost/Selling Price	Number Sold	Total Cost	Total Sales
Hamburger	$1.99/$7.50	65	$129.35	$487.50
Salad	$1.23/$6.75	48	$59.03	$324.00
Pizza	$1.01/$3.95	89	$89.89	$351.55
Tuna sandwich	$1.87/$6.25	67	$125.29	$418.75
Total		269	$403.56	$1,581.80
	Average contribution margin: $4.38	Average variable rate: 25.51%	Average variable cost: $1.50	Average check: $5.88

ANSWERS TO WORKBOOK PROBLEMS

1. a. S = sales: VC + CM
   b. VC = variable costs: S – CM
   c. FC = fixed costs: CM – P
   d. P = profit: CM – FC
   e. CR = contribution rate: 1 – VR or CM / S
   f. VR = variable rate: VC / S or 1 – CR
   g. CM = contribution margin: FC + P
2. S = VC + CM
   CM = S – VC
   P = CM – FC or FC – VC
3. FC = P – S = VC
   VC = P – S + FC
   S = P + VC + FC
4. $500
5. $1,600
6. $1,000
7. 2,400
8. 2,900
9. a. .25
   b. .75
10. CM = FC + P: $11,000
11. CM / S = CR
    $11,000 / $25,000 = .44
12. a. CR = 1 – VR, or .44
    b. VR = 1 – CR, or .56

13. a. Sales = \$10,000
    b. CM = \$5,000
    c. CR = .50
    d. VR = .50
14. VR = \$10,000 / \$15,000, or .67
15. a. \$13,235
    b. $P = S \times CR - FC$ = \$3,150
16.

Sales in Units	AC	AVC	FC	P
100	\$14	\$4	\$1,000	0
120	\$19	\$4	\$1,800	0
1,125	\$11	\$3	\$6,000	\$3,000
1,636.4	\$17	\$6	\$18,000	0
2,875	\$16	\$8	\$23,000	0
4,000	\$14	\$7	\$29,000	\$1,000
21,000	\$14	\$6	\$168,000	0
26,636.4	\$14	\$3	\$293,000	0

5

Controls in Food Purchasing

CHAPTER OBJECTIVES

After finishing this chapter the students will be able to:

- Define and utilize food purchasing terminology
- Differentiate among the three purchasing standards
- View forms associated with purchasing
- Describe the different purchasing methods
- Use formulas including:
  - Periodic ordering amount
  - Perpetual ordering amount
  - As purchased (AP) calculations
  - Edible portion (EP) for both food quantity and food cost

ANSWERS TO TEXT PROBLEMS

1. A product specification is a listing of all the criteria about ingredients and supplies. This will comprise information about the product's grade, color, size and place of origin, to name a few. A purchase specification includes all of the additional information about receiving the product into the establishment, including delivery instructions, compatibility requirements, and credit terms.
2. Yield percent is a factor used to ensure that the proper amount is purchased, and to calculate EP cost.
3. | Advantage | Disadvantage |
   |---|---|
   | Generally lower prices per dollar volume | Who determines the costs? |
   | Do not have to get quotes | Only one relationship with supplier |
4. It determines how much of the product will be available for the intended use.
5. This figure is the amount purchased as compared to the edible portion after trimming.
6. Specifications, hands-on calculations, and manufacturers estimate.
7. 83 lb. 5 1/3 oz.
8. $1.25 per pound or $104.17
9. 4 gallons, 3 quarts, and 23 1/2 ounces
10. $0.69
11. $0.53
12. Buy 125.74 pounds of steak, 57 pounds of potatoes, 52.78 pounds of beans, and sell for $26.40.
13. To ensure that the correct product is purchased at the correct price.
14. Answers will vary.
15. The sheet is sent out to let distributors know how much of each product is needed.

16. In the perpetual method, the quantity of product that can be ordered remains the same, but the order dates change, fluctuating around the needs of buyer. In the periodic method, the order dates are set at consistent intervals, and order quantities change according to the amount needed at the preset order time.
17. Physical inventory is the actual counting of items, and perpetual inventory is the on-going theoretical count of what should be in inventory.
18. (14×4) $56 + 12 = 68 - 8 = 60$
19. (14×3) $42 + 6 = 48 - 5 = 43$ or 8 units
20. 8
+2 safety stock
Reorder point: 10 cans
43
−10
33
+ 8 delivery
Order amount: 41 cans
21. $100 - 12 = 88 + 6 = 94$ or 16 units
22. (6×4) $24 - 10 = 14$ $+ 6 = 20$ cans
23. $200 - 42 = 158 + 21 = 179$ or 8 cases

ANSWERS TO WORKBOOK PROBLEMS

1. 1. Who is the clientele?
   2. Decide on a concept.
   3. Establish standards/expenditures.
   4. Purchase food.
2. a. Quantity
   b. Quality
   c. Price
3. a. Criteria of a product
   b. additional information such as delivery, compatibility, credit
   c. consistent intervals of ordering with changing amounts
   d. when inventory reaches this level we order more products
   e. quantity the same, dates change
   f. amount to cover emergencies
   g. on-going
   h. all products physically counted
4. 50 lbs.
5. 130 lbs.
6. Amount to Order:
   30 lbs.
   5 1/2 boxes
   210 steaks
   19 gal.
   35 pieces

7. a. specific items needed—take bids from companies—but best price
   b. list of products and a place for inventory, par, amount required, and a place for bids
   c. no one aware of others' bid
   d. supplier's price plus an agreed mark-up percentage
   e. many users combine for the best price and product
   f. gets all they can from one purveyor
   g. gets all of product for a period of time after negotiation
   h. goes to warehouse and get food products
   i. delivery of same product at some time interval
   j. companies with multiple properties
   k. purchased online
   l. amount usable for producing recipe
   m. amount usable and the nonusable amount
   n. the % of a product that is usable

8.

Product	EP	AP	Yield %
Beef, ground	20 lbs.	**26.6 lbs.**	75%
Lettuce	**65 lbs.**	100 lbs.	65%
Tomatoes	50 lbs.	**51.5 lbs.**	97%
Steaks	**90 lbs.**	100 lbs.	90%
Pork chops	4 oz.	5 oz.	**80%**

9.

EP cost	AP cost	Yield
$24.00	$12.00	50%
$170.00	$128.00	75%
$33.09	$22.50	68%
$8.00	$16.00	**50%**
$100.00	**$70.00**	70%
$228.00	**$159.60**	70%

10. a. 218.75 lbs.
    b. 205.88 lbs.
    c. 194.44 lbs.

11. Buy a, b, and c

6

Controls in Food Receiving, Storage, and Issuing

CHAPTER OBJECTIVES

After finishing this chapter the students will be able to:

- Understand product terminology connected with the flow of food
- Differentiate among the three receiving standards
- Understand receiving techniques
- Understand storage principles
- Differentiate between directs and stores
- Understand issuing practices
- Calculate the value of inventory via different methods, including:
  - FIFO
  - LIFO
  - Weighted average
  - Last purchase price
  - Actual price
- Use formulas including: Average inventory and inventory turnover

ANSWERS TO TEXT PROBLEMS

1. A receiving sheet is a checks and balances for large operations to ensure that all deliveries are accounted for.
2. Directs are products that go directly to the department that utilizes them, and bypass the storeroom both physically and for accounting purposes. Stores get put into the warehouse and the products are distributed as needed. At a later date when the products are requested and delivered, the charges are transferred to the department requesting them.
3. Quantity the same as ordered, quality the same as ordered, and price the same as ordered.
4. FIFO storage practices mean that the actual inventory is rotated and the first products in are the first products out. FIFO inventory control is placing a value on the items in inventory based on how many are left and the cost associated with the most recent purchases of the items.

5.

	Value of Closing Inventory	Cost of Food Issued
FIFO	$30.86	$20.02
LIFO	$31.26	$19.62
Actual	Cannot determine	Cannot determine
Latest Purchase Price	$31.02	$19.86
Weighted Price	$31.09	$19.79

6. Answers will vary.
7. 2.63 times that period.
8. Answers will vary.
9.

	Ending Inventory Value	Cost of Food Issued
FIFO	$103.68	$334.05
LIFO	$99.57	$338.16
Actual	Cannot determine	Cannot determine
Latest Purchase Price	$102.00	$335.73
Weighted Price	$102.96	$334.77

10. 20.72
11. Quality, quantity, and cost standards
12. Improved quality and shelf life
13.

	Ending Inventory Value	Cost of Food Issued
FIFO	$46.50	$105.75
LIFO	$48.20	$104.05
Actual	Cannot determine	Cannot determine
Latest Purchase Price	$45.60	$106.65
Weighted Price	$48.00	$104.25

14. 20–25 times per year
15. 150 times per year

ANSWERS TO WORKBOOK PROBLEMS

1. Receiving Standards = quality, quantity, and cost
2. a. specifications
   b. amount; received
   c. prices
   d. receiving
   e. FIFO
   f. 34–38°F
   g. warehouse requisition
   h. Similar
3. a. stores
   b. perishables
4. Monthly
5. b. That one is consistent
6. 20–25; 7–12
   Per week? .4–.5
   Per month? 1.7–2.1
7.

OI	CI	Purchased	AI	IT
$12,000	$12,000	$15,000	**$12,000**	**1.25**
$16,500	$17,000	$31,000	**$16,750**	**1.82**
$22,000	$23,000	$45,000	**$22,050**	**0.5**
$6,000	$5,000	$18,000	**$5,500**	**0.29**
$12,380	$6,380	$23,000	**$9,380**	**3.09**
$31,000	$31,200	$103,000	**$31,100**	**3.30**
$15,000	$14,000	$93,000	**$14,500**	**6.48**

8. Fill in the chart for valuation of an inventory.

Product	Unit	Jan. 1 Amt	Jan. 1 Price	Jan. 12 Amt	Jan. 12 Price	Jan. 15 Amt	Jan. 15 Price	Jan. 30 Amt	Jan. 30 Price	O I	C I	LIFO	FIFO	Average Price	Last Price
a) lettuce	lbs.	55	$.50	10	$.55	10	$.50	20	$.60	25	30 lbs.	**$15.00**	**$17.00**	**$16.13**	**$18.00**
b) tomatoes	Each	60	$1	50	$1	50	$1.20	120	$1	50	50	**$50.00**	**$50.00**	**$52.50**	**$50.00**
c) cheese	lbs.	10	$2	10	$2	10	$2.50	20	$2.50	70	80 lbs.	**$155.00**	**$155.00**	**$180.00**	**$200.00**
d) taco shells	Each	100	$.10	100	$.10	100	$.15	200	$.15	80	100	**$10.00**	**$15.00**	**$12.50**	**$15.00**
e) hamburger	lbs.	50	$2	50	$2.50	50	$2	50	$2	50	40	**$80.00**	**$80.00**	**$85.00**	**$80.00**
f) seasoning	can	1	$1	1	$.75	2	$1	0	$.75	1	3	**$2.65**	**$2.75**	**$2.63**	**$2.25**

9. a. Food cost for October? $6,800
   b. Food cost percentage? 42.50%
   c. Opening inventory = $900
   d. AI = $800 IT = .12

10.

LIFO Method	FIFO Method
12 cans @ $13.20	6 cans @ $1.50 = $9.00
6 cans @ $7.20	12 cans @ $1.30 = $15.60
1 can @ $1.30	1 can @ $1.20 = $1.20
19 cans @ $21.70	19 cans @ $25.80

If you use LIFO you have on inventory the first cans. $21.70 is a smaller inventory. You pay less taxes on a smaller inventory.

7

Controls in Food Production

CHAPTER OBJECTIVES

After finishing this chapter the students will be able to:

- Understand the need and usage of a production schedule
- Understand the need and usage of a standardized recipe
- Understand the need and usage of a standard portion size including:
  - Volume
  - Count
  - Weight
- Calculate the standard portion cost
- Understand the concept of yield factor/percent
- Complete a butcher's yield and a cooking loss test
- Evaluate causes of over-/under-production
- Calculate daily and to-date food costs
- Understand the concept of potential savings

ANSWERS TO TEXT PROBLEMS

1. Food cost for short periods of time may give false statistics, compared to those that are created from longer time periods.
2.

Date	Direct	Stores	Transfers In	Transfers Out	Sales	Sales to Date	FC Today	FC to Date	FC % Today	FC % to Date
8/1	$128	$1,387	$32	$29	$3,678	$3,678	$1,518	$1,518	41.27	41.27
8/2	0	$923	$65	$46	$3,385	$7,063	$942	$2,460	27.83	34.83
8/3	$76	$690	$28	$34	$2,840	$9,903	$760	$3,220	26.76	32.52

3.

Date	Direct	Stores	Transfers In	Transfers Out	Sales	Sales to Date	FC Today	FC to Date	FC % Today	FC % to Date
3/1	$1,598	$3,292	$160	$67	$12,490	$12,490	$4,983	$4,983	39.90	39.90
3/2	$990	$2,310	$18	$150	$9,811	$22,301	$3,168	$8,151	32.29	36.55
3/3	$22	$1,690	0	$26	$9,280	$31,581	$1,686	$9,837	18.17	31.15

4.

Butcher's Yield
Item: Prime Rib — Total cost: $169.75
Pieces: 1 — Weight: 25 lb.
Grade: U.S. Choice — Price per pound: $6.79

Breakdown	Weight Lb.	Oz.	Weight (in decimal)	Ratio to Total Pound	Value per Pound	Total Value	Usable Pound	Multiplier per Pound
Fat	2	4	2.25	9%	$0.15	$0.34		
Bones	1	0	1.00	4%	$0.79	$0.79		
Short ribs	1	4	1.25	5%	$4.46	$5.58		
Ground beef	0	12	0.75	3%	$1.39	$1.04		
Loss in cutting	0	4	0.75	1%				
Prime rib	19	8	19.50	78%		$162.00	$8.31	1.22
Total	25	0	25.00	100%	$6.79	$169.75		

5.

Breakdown	Weight Lb.	Oz.	Weight (in decimal)	Ratio to Total Pound	Value per Pound	Total Value	Usable Pound	Multiplier per Pound
Original weight	25	0	25.00	100%	$6.79	$169.75		
Trimmed weight	19	8	19.50	78%	$8.31	$162.01		
Byproducts	5	8	5.50	22%				
Cooked weight	18	4	18.25	73%				
Loss in cooking	1	4	1.25	5%				
Bones and trim	0	12	0.75	3%				
Saleable weight	17	8	17.50	70%		$162.01	$9.26	1.36

6. $4.63
7. $18.52
8. $9.51
9. $19.04
10. 94.5 lb. / .70 = 135 lb.
11. Answers will vary, but should include the need to know edible portion and edible portion cost.
12. The total cost of the meat is divided by the number of main items produced. The remaining by-products are considered free.
13. Answers will vary.
14. A food production schedule will ensure that the proper amount of product is prepared and will aid in accounting for food products.
15. Standard portion cost is what the menu item should cost to prepare. It is calculated by management's interpretation of the three standards.
16. Weight (10 oz. N.Y. Strip), volume (6 oz. soup), and count (6 shrimp)
17. $2.22
18. 8–9 pieces of shrimp costing $4.50, and selling for $16.07
19. It costs $0.30, and sells for $1.36
20. It costs $0.48, and sells for $2.18
21. $7.08
22. 174 filets
23. Chicken breast: $8.21
    Tomato sauce: $1.87
    Mozzarella cheese: $3.75
    Total for 10 people: $13.83
24. Onion: $1.47
    Butter: $0.93
    Beef stock: $5.30
    Total for soup: $7.70
    21 portions each at $0.37
    Garnish cost for bread $0.07, for cheese $0.25
    Total cost: $0.67
25. $1.54

26.

Butcher's Yield							
Item: Prime Rib			Total cost: $397.51				
Pieces: 1			Weight: 73 lb. 12 oz.				
Grade: U.S. Choice			Price per pound: $5.39			$73.75	
Breakdown	**Weight Lb. Oz.**	**Weight (in decimal)**	**Ratio to Total Pound**	**Value per Pound**	**Total Value**	**Usable Pound**	**Multiplier per Pound**
Fat	12 4	12.25	16.61%	$0.09	$1.10		
Bones	7 8	7.50	10.17%	$0.93	$6.98		
Short ribs	3 12	3.75	5.08%	$3.09	$11.59		
Ground beef	4 4	4.25	5.76%	$1.19	$5.06		
Loss in cutting	0 8	0.50	0.68%				
Prime rib	45 8	45.50	61.69%		$372.79	$8.19	1.52
Total	75 12	73.75	100%	$5.39	$397.51		

Cooking Loss Test							
Breakdown	**Weight Lb. Oz.**	**Weight (in decimal)**	**Ratio to Total Pound**	**Value per Pound**	**Total Value**	**Usable Pound**	**Multiplier per Pound**
Original weight	75 12	73.75	100%	$5.39	$397.51		
Trimmed weight	45 8	45.50	61.69%	$8.19	$372.79		
Byproducts	28 4	28.25	38.31%				
Cooked weight	41 12	41.75	56.61%				
Loss in cooking	3 12	3.75	5.08%				
Bones and trim	3 0	3.00	4.07%				
Saleable weight	38 12	38.75	52.54%		$372.79	$9.62	1.78

620 oz. / 10 oz. = 62 servings
2250 oz. / .5254 = 4282.45 / 16 = 267 lb. 10 1/2 oz.
9.62 × .625 = $6.00
5.99 × 1.78 = $10.66

27.

Butcher's Yield Item: Veal Pieces: 1 Grade: U.S. Choice			Total cost: $163.59 Weight: 41 lb. Price per pound: $3.99					
Breakdown	**Weight Lb.**	**Oz.**	**Weight (in decimal)**	**Ratio to Total Pound**	**Value per Pound**	**Total Value**	**Usable Pound**	**Multiplier per Pound**
Fat	2	0	2.0000	4.88%	$0.18	$0.36		
Bones	5	3	5.1875	12.65%	$1.99	$10.32		
Stew	3	11	3.6875	8.99%	$3.99	$14.71		
Veal cutlet	30	2	30.1250	73.48%		$138.19	$4.59	1.15
Total	41	0	41.0000	100%	$3.99	$163.59		

28. 199 lb. 1/2 oz.

ANSWERS TO WORKBOOK PROBLEMS

1. Forecasts
2.

Steaks	% of sales	Mon.	Tues.	Wed.	Thurs.	Fri.	Sat.	Sun.	Total per week
Filets 8 oz.	21	**63**	**63**	**73.5**	**84**	**105**	**126**	**147**	**661.5**
Filets 10 oz.	12	**36**	**36**	**42**	**48**	**60**	**72**	**84**	**378**
Rib Eye 10 oz.	18	**54**	**54**	**63**	**72**	**90**	**108**	**126**	**567**
Rib Eye 19 oz.	6	**18**	**18**	**21**	**24**	**30**	**36**	**42**	**189**
Strip Steak 18 oz.	21	**63**	**63**	**73.5**	**84**	**105**	**126**	**147**	**661.5**
Round Steak 18 oz.	3	**9**	**9**	**10.5**	**12**	**15**	**18**	**21**	**94.5**
Chicken Fried Steak 6 oz.	12	**36**	**36**	**42**	**48**	**60**	**72**	**84**	**378**
T-Bone Steak 22 oz.	4	**12**	**12**	**14**	**16**	**20**	**24**	**28**	**126**
T-Bone Steak 12 oz.	3	**9**	**9**	**10.5**	**12**	**15**	**18**	**21**	**94.5**
Forecast		300	300	350	400	500	600	700	

3.

Ingredients	Quantity	Price	Unit Cost	Ingredient Cost
Ground beef	12 lbs.	$2.10 per lb.	**$2.10 per lb.**	**$25.20**
Slightly beaten egg	5	$0.84 per dozen	**$0.07 per egg**	**$0.35**
Minced onion	2 ozs.	$0.37 per lb.	**$0.23 per oz.**	**$0.05**
Salt	2 ozs.	$0.16 per lb.	**$0.01 per oz.**	**$0.02**
Pepper	1 oz.	$2.56 per lb.	**$0.16 per oz.**	**$0.16**
Beef stock	1 gal.	$0.60 per gal.	**$0.60 per gal.**	**$0.60**
Bread crumbs	1 lb.	$0.30 per lb.	**$0.30 per lb.**	**$0.30**

Total Recipe Cost = **$26.68**
Per-Portion Cost = **$0.534**

4. Price, accuracy, knowledge, by-product use, area available, skill
5. $0
6. Pork loin
7. a. What is the % of usable product? 65%
   b. What is the true cost of the EP? $3.07/lb.
   c. What is the ratio of fat to total weight? 2 / 10
   d. What is the ratio of fat to EP? 2 / 6.5
8. Fill in the blanks:

Description	Cost per Case	Weight per Case (lbs.)	Waste per Case (lbs.)	Usable Lettuce per Case (lbs.)	Processing Cost of Labor	Total Cost	Price per lb. of EP
Head Lettuce	$15.35	50 3/4	23 3/4	**27**	$2.35	$17.70	**$.66**
Trimmed Lettuce	$14.35	28 3/4	4 1/2	**24.25**	$0.95	$15.30	**$.63**
Cleaned and Cored Lettuce	$15.10	26 1/2	0	**26.5**	$0.78	$15.88	**$.59**
Pre-cut Salad Mix	$9.85	20	0	**20**	$0.00	$9.85	**$.49**

a. Which lettuce is the best buy considering all the above? Precut
b. What else could be considered along with the price? Labor, trash, cleanup, sanitation, by-products

9. Fill in the blanks:

Carrots	AP Wt. (lbs.)	Price lbs.	EP (lbs.)	Yield % Amount	Effective Price/ lb. of EP Carrot
Type A	100	$.06	75	**75**	**$.08**
Type B	100	$.08	80	**80**	**$.10**
Type C	30	$.10	30	**100**	**$.10**

a. Which carrot type would be the best to buy? Type A
b. What else could be considered in buying carrots from the above choices? Labor, cleanup, sanitation, by-products

10.

Size of Roast	18 lbs.	20 lbs.	22 lbs.	25 lbs.
% of Loss:	X	X	X	X
16%	**15** EP lbs.	**16.8** EP lbs.	X	X
18%	X	X	**18.4** EP lbs.	X
22%	X	X	X	**19.5** EP lbs.
Price per Pound	$2.12	$2.00	$1.95	$1.92
Total Price AP	**$38.16**	**$40.00**	**$40.95**	**$48.00**
Price EP per lb.	**$2.51**	**$2.38**	**$2.22**	**$2.46**

11.

Amount of Item	Item Ingredients	Cost	SP if D FC % = 25%	SP if D FC = 30%
8 ozs.	Soup	$0.21	**.84**	**.70**
6 ozs.	Chicken ala Metro	$1.10	**4.40**	**3.67**
4 ozs.	Salad	$0.62	**2.48**	**2.07**
3 ozs.	Vegetable	$0.40	**1.60**	**1.33**
3 ozs.	Rice Pilaf	$0.18	**.77**	**.60**

Recalculate using the following portions:

6 ozs.	Soup		**.63**	**.53**
4 ozs.	Chicken ala Metro		**2.93**	**2.44**
6 ozs.	Salad		**3.72**	**3.11**
4 ozs.	Vegetable		**2.13**	**1.77**
6 ozs.	Rice Pilaf		**1.44**	**1.20**

12.

	Revenue	Direct Deliveries	Storeroom Usage	In	Out	Employee Meals	CF Today	CF Today %	This Week to Date Cost	This Week to Date FC %
Day 1	$500	$200	$10	$15	$20	$20	a	b	c	d
Day 2	$350	$100	$0	$10	$10	$20	e	f	g	h
Day 3	$600	$300	$0	$0	$0	$20	i	j	k	l

Show for each value of:	Formula used:
a. **$185**	**$200 + $10 + $15 – $20 = $185**
b. **37%**	**$185 / $500**
c. **$185**	**$200 + $10 + $15 – $20 = $185**
d. **37%**	**$185 / $500**
e. **$80**	**$100 + $10 – $10 –$20 = $80**
f. **22.9%**	**$80 / $350**
g. **$265**	**$185 + $80 = $265**
h. **31.2%**	**$265 / $850**
i. **$2.80**	**$300 – $20 = $280**
j. **46.7%**	**$280 / $60**
k. **$530**	**$185 + $80 + $265 = $530**
l. **36.5%**	**$530 / $1,450**

13.

	Purchased Weight	Unusable Product	Purchased Price / lb.	Ratio to Total Weight	EP Price/ lb.	Total Cost
Turkey Whole	24 lbs.		$.72			$17.28
Bones/fat		4 lbs.		**16.7%**		
Cooking loss		7 lbs.		**29.2%**		
EP turkey		**13 lbs.**		**54.2%**	**$1.33**	**$17.28**
BSFCT						
EP turkey	16 lbs.	16 lbs.	$1.20		**$1.20**	

a. The best buy is the BSFCT.

14. Cut your own—not considering labor
15. The precut steaks

8

Controls in Beverage Purchasing, Receiving, and Issuing

CHAPTER OBJECTIVES

After finishing this chapter the students will be able to:

- Identify the differences between a license and control state
- Identify various alcoholic beverages within the three classifications
- Identify purchasing standards
- Differentiate among the three receiving standards
- Distinguish receiving techniques
- Distinguish storage principles
- Distinguish issuing practices
- Give overview of non-alcoholic beverage purchasing

ANSWERS TO TEXT PROBLEMS

1. The average inventory turnover rate for wine is indeterminable.
2. The average inventory turnover rate for spirits is 18.
3. The average inventory turnover rate for beer is 24.
4. Answers may vary, but should include no competition.
5. Answers may vary, but should include credit, competition, and delivery.
6. Answers may vary, but should include stock requisitions, check points, bottle trades, and limited access.
7. Answers will vary.
8. Answers will vary.
9. When purchasing alcohol, you may buy broken cases.
10. It is usually the least expensive per volume amount. and usually gives a higher yield percent.
11. The cost of beverage issued in the example is $132,548.
12. 2.08
13. An equipment program is when a supplier provides equipment as long as you purchase their product for use in the machine (i.e., coffee maker when you buy a brand of coffee).

14. Stored at an angle, 75 percent humidity, varied temperatures.
15. Storage principles for bottled and canned beers are room temperature, FIFO, three-month shelf life. Keg beer is not pasteurized so it should be refrigerated with a shelf life of one month.
16. Shelf stable, no refrigeration needed.

ANSWERS TO WORKBOOK PROBLEMS

(Chapters 8 and 9 are together)

1. Define:
   a. Delivered, negotiation of price, credit, distributor license
   b. No credit, no delivery, no price negotiation, strict control over alcohol sales
   c. One distributor and brand
2. cost
3. FIFO
4. little
5.

	OI	CI	Cost	AI	IT
Beer	$3,280	$3,161	$6,100	**$3,220.50**	**.53**
Wine	$6,150	$4,250	$7,200	**$5,200**	**.72**
Spirits	$2,394	$3,671	$3,500	**$3,032.50**	**.87**

6.

	Sales	OI	CI	Cost	BC	BC%	AI	IT
Bar 1	$180,250	$15,000	$14,280	$16,200	**$16,920**	**9**	**$14,640**	**1.15**
Bar 2	$179,330	$16,390	$16,300	$18,300	**$18,390**	**10**	**$16,345**	**1.12**
Bar 3	$391,000	$20,120	$18,200	$17,200	**$19,120**	**4.9**	**$19,160**	**1.00**

7. .222
8. $577.20

9.

	Sales	OI	CI	Cost
Beer	$2,000	$5,800	**$3,800**	**1**
Wine	$12,000	$23,000	**$9,000**	**8**
Liquor	$13,000	$31,000	**$18,000**	**9**
Non-alcoholic	$18,000	$87,000	**$69,000**	**12**
TOTALS	**$45,000**	**$146,800**	**$99,800**	

a. Which is the best profit maker? Non-alcoholic

10. 16.70%
11. $300
12. $300
13. 15%
14. 25.7%

9

Controls in Beverage Production

CHAPTER OBJECTIVES

After finishing this chapter the students will be able to:

- Distinguish the value of beverage production control
- Differentiate among different bars
- Distinguish between different glassware and the value of this in beverage production
- Identify different production controls
- Calculate beverage inventory
- Identify government controls for beverages
- Explain dramshop laws
- Differentiate between well brands and call brands
- Identify different methods of inventory valuation
- Evaluate the positives and negatives of extensive wine service

ANSWERS TO TEXT PROBLEMS

1. Answers will vary.
2. Answers may vary, but the pros should include extended customer base, higher profits, and prestige. Cons should include an outlay for product, storage, and training.
3. Bottle size may change from one bar to another due to ease of use, visual appeal, and cost control.
4. Issuing control is a major factor in the beverage industry because it has a strong potential for financial abuse.
5. Answers will vary.
6. A standardized recipe is a recipe that can be followed consistently by most people.
7. Glass size is important for the standardized recipe and portion control.
8. Free pour is considered a limited control technique because it does not ensure accuracy and compliance by employees, even if they are trained in free pour.
9. Pros: Every drink is mixed the same, sales system is attached to the machine, ease for high volume. Cons: Poor impression on customers, if it breaks you are out sales.
10. Under pouring, comp sales, leaving cash drawer open, rigging spouts, faking broken bottle.
11. Some government controls over alcohol are purchase control (control vs. license), financial investment (escrow account), financial record keeping of sales and purchases (strict control of wholesale sales to control tax receipts), licensure of employees (background check).

12. Dramshop laws are third-party liability laws making an owner/server liable if someone they serve alcohol to has an accident. Answers may vary on whether or not your state has dramshop laws.
13. Well brands, named after the well they sit in, are management-chosen brands used when no brand is specified. Call brands are when a specific brand is ordered.
14. Three methods of monitoring beverage operations are:
    a. *liquid measure approach*—an exact measurement of every bottle is taken to calculate expected sales
    b. *sales value approach*—each bottle should generate a specific amount of sales
    c. *cost approach*—OI + P – CI = COBI
15. Answer will vary.
16. The beverage differential is the difference in sales value of a bottle if sold as straight shots, as compared to mixed drinks.

ANSWERS TO WORKBOOK PROBLEMS

(Chapters 8 and 9 are together)

1. Define:
    a. Delivered, negotiation of price, credit, distributor license
    b. No credit, no delivery, no price negotiation, strict control over alcohol sales
    c. One distributor and brand
2. cost
3. FIFO
4. little
5.

	OI	CI	Cost	AI	IT
Beer	$3,280	$3,161	$6,100	**$3,220.50**	**.53**
Wine	$6,150	$4,250	$7,200	**$5,200**	**.72**
Spirits	$2,394	$3,671	$3,500	**$3,032.50**	**.87**

6.

	Sales	OI	CI	Cost	BC	BC%	AI	IT
Bar 1	$180,250	$15,000	$14,280	$16,200	**$16,920**	**9**	**$14,640**	**1.15**
Bar 2	$179,330	$16,390	$16,300	$18,300	**$18,390**	**10**	**$16,345**	**1.12**
Bar 3	$391,000	$20,120	$18,200	$17,200	**$19,120**	**4.9**	**$19,160**	**1.00**

7. .222
8. $577.20

9.

	Sales	OI	CI	Cost
Beer	$2,000	$5,800	**$3,800**	**1**
Wine	$12,000	$23,000	**$9,000**	**8**
Liquor	$13,000	$31,000	**$18,000**	**9**
Non-alcoholic	$18,000	$87,000	**$69,000**	**12**
TOTALS	**$45,000**	**$146,800**	**$99,800**	

a. Which is the best profit maker? Non-alcoholic

10. 16.70%
11. $300
12. $300
13. 15%
14. 25.7%

10

Costs in Labor

CHAPTER OBJECTIVES

After finishing this chapter the students will be able to:

- Differentiate among the salaried and hourly employees
- Describe the high turnover rate in the industry and some methods to lower it
- Describe the costs associated with high employee turnover
- Explain ways to save labor dollars
- Calculate labor cost percent
- Examine forecasting for labor needs
- Use an operating budget
- Explore various compensation techniques

ANSWERS TO TEXT PROBLEMS

1. Current (received shortly after performing duties): Taxes, insurance, paid holidays, educational assistance, concierge service, exercise facility, childcare, meals, flexible schedules, telecommuting, moving expenses, signing bonus, housing, low interest loans

   Deferred (received in the future, usually after separation of employment): Golden parachutes, low interest loans
2. Direct (given directly to employee): Taxes, moving expenses, signing bonus

   Indirect (not directly given to employee in a paycheck): Insurance, paid holidays, educational assistance, concierge service, exercise facility, childcare, meals, flexible schedules, telecommuting, housing, low interest loans, golden parachutes
3. Answers will vary, but should include varied business rush periods, seasonal work, better control of labor, and benefits.
4. Answers will vary, but should include that FLSA affects every business, and since many hospitality operations are open 24/7, the need for employees during all hours of operation creates more overtime opportunities.
5. Hiring outside companies to perform non-critical components of an operation.
6. Controls costs, provides financial efficiency, and eliminates cash drain.
   Strengthens employment capacity without increasing personnel
   Offers access to experts with skills and expertise, and new technologies immediately
   Focus on their core business objectives
7. Use of employees, cost
8. Improper training, many opportunities
9. Proper training

10. Over 40 hours in a consecutive 7-day/24-hour period
11. Answers will vary, but should include workflow design and equipment.
12. Answers will vary, but should include workflow design, equipment, and menu planning.
13. Answers will vary.
14. Their salary does not change with an increase in business.
15. When food cost is high, labor cost will usually decrease, and vice versa.
16. A percentage of employees that leave to the number of positions.
17. Without forecasting, correct scheduling is hard to do.

ANSWERS TO WORKBOOK PROBLEMS

1.

Friday, June 10 Labor	**Forecasted Hours**	**Actual Hours**	**Variance**	**Cost of Variance**	**Rate/hr.**	**Total Pay**
Dishwashers	35	35	**0**	**0**	$6.50	**$227.50**
Cooks	50	55	**+5**	**$60**	$12.00	**$660.00**
Servers	40	43	**+3**	**$9.75**	$3.25	**$139.75**
Busers	15	12	**-3**	**$16.05**	$5.35	**$64.20**
Management	16	20	**+4**	**$72.00**	$18.00	**$360.00**
Totals	**156**	**165**	**+9**	**$125.70**		**$1,451.45**

2. Additional $30—Make OLC = $1,481.45
3. Training, costs of rehiring, find, replace
4. a. deferred compensation: Deferred until a future time
   b. current compensation: Paid in current time period
   c. direct compensation: Paid directly to the employee
   d. indirect compensation: Paid, but not immediately to employee

11

Controls in Labor

CHAPTER OBJECTIVES

After finishing this chapter the students will be able to:

- Differentiate between varieties of quality standards
- Differentiate between varieties of quantity standards
- Evaluate the cost standard of labor
- Distinguish between the hospitality industry and other industries with regard to productivity standards
- Use an organizational chart
- Differentiate between a job analysis and a job description
- Identify appropriate corrective actions

ANSWERS TO TEXT PROBLEMS

1. Answers will vary depending on what jobs are listed.
2. It will show management the needs–assessment for the property, including front and back of the house, support positions, and outsourcing.
3. Decides which tasks should be performed in-house, and which will be outsourced.
4. It details jobs and their descriptions.
5. Answers can vary, but might include accountability—job descriptions and responsibilities allow management to ensure that efficiency in labor is in place.
6. A task analysis will detail the specific needs of a job, and then allows a job description to be created that fulfills those needs.
7. Answers will vary, but might include the needs of the clientele, the economy, and union influence.
8. Answers will vary.
9. Answers will vary.
10. Answers will vary.
11. Answers will vary.
12. Answers will vary.
13. External observation of employees.

ANSWERS TO WORKBOOK PROBLEMS

1. Total cost of labor/sales
2. Quality, quantity, costs
3. Productivity
4. Teach standards and train to meet standards

5. a. Task analysis: What, when, and how work needs to be done
   b. Cost benefit analysis: What tasks need to be done in house and what to outsource
   c. Job description: Define what jobs need to be done, and qualifications needed
   d. Job specification: What duties are assigned to a job
   e. Quality standard: Experience and training needed
   f. Quantity standard: Amount of work an employee should do in a time period
   g. Cost standards: Pay more for experience and trained staff
   h. Productivity: Amount of work produced in a given time period

6.

Task	Possible Outsourced	Positive and Negative Effect on Quality	Effect on Costs
1	**Payroll**	**Loss of control**	**Can cut costs**
2	**Equipment repairs**	**More timely repairs and can increase quality**	**Can cut costs**
3			
4			
5			
6			
7			
8			
9			

7. Consider the following:

Hour	Food Costs	Labor Costs	Benefits	Sales	Total Labor Costs	Profit
1	$100	$100	$10	$300	**$110**	**$90**
2	$200	$100	$10	$400	**$110**	**$90**
3	$200	$200	$25	$400	**$225**	**($25)**
4	$300	$150	$10	$700	**$160**	**$240**

a. Which hour did you make the most profit? Hour #4
b. What is the lowest labor cost % (LC%) per hour? Why? Hours 1 and 2
c.

Hour	LC %
1	**30**
2	**27.5**
3	**56.25**
4	**22.9**

d. Either high sales or low labor costs in dollars

8. a. It is very hard to be "fair." Scheduling is time consuming.
9. a. labor cost: $1,225
   b. labor cost %: 39.20%
   c. food cost: $1,200
   d. food cost %: 37.50%

12

Controls for Other Expenses

CHAPTER OBJECTIVES

After finishing this chapter the students will be able to:

- Identify controllable and non-controllable costs associated with
  - Restaurant operations
  - Business operations
  - Facilities
  - Occupancy

ANSWERS TO TEXT PROBLEMS

1. Costs associated with restaurant operations:
   a. Linens—Do you need them or not? Buy and clean them in-house or rent?
   b. Flatware—Which weight, pattern, pieces, silver or stainless steel?
   c. Decorations—Use fresh or fake flowers? Hang originals or copies of paintings?
   d. Cleaning supplies—Safety, sanitation, and proper training of employees on how to use them can keep costs down
   e. Utilities—Checking thermostats regularly, checking equipment for proper operations
   f. Menus—Use leather-bound, board, or laminated menus?
   g. Franchise fees—Upfront money or percentage of sales?
   h. Product tasting—Research and development of new products
   i. Outsourced services—Pest control, trash removal, valet services
2. Costs associated with business operations:
   a. Licenses—Permits (special uses, signs, building, health); licenses (liquor, business, vending machine)
   b. Marketing—Free meals, mailers, newspaper advertisements, coupons, television ads
   c. Music and entertainment—Live or canned, royalties
   d. Office expenses—Personnel, office space
3. Costs associated with facilities:
   a. Furniture, fixtures, used or new equipment, maintenance of FFEs

4. Costs associated with occupancy:
   a. Land and building ownership—Free standing, attached, leasing land and/or building
   b. Rent—Building (fixed cost or variable percentage of sales)
   c. Insurance—Workmen's compensation, property
   d. Landscape—Employee maintained or outsourced
   e. Parking lot—Valet, liabilities, upkeep
   f. Building maintenance—Windows, snow removal, signage, safety
   g. Taxes and legislation—Local, state, federal, lobbyists
5. Minimize restaurant operations costs by
   a. Use butcher block paper over linens, do not use linens.
   b. Choose flatware appropriate for your establishment.
   c. Use copies of famous paintings and fake flowers.
   d. Utilities: Monitor equipment and thermostats.
   e. Menu: Use reusable laminated if appropriate.
   f. Fees: Do the benefits outweigh the fees?
   g. Can products can be tested at a corporate level? Limit your changes.
   h. Outsourced services: Don't outsource if the job can be done in-house cheaply.
6. Minimize business operation costs
   a. Marketing—Research who your clientele is and market around that.
   b. Music and entertainment—Less cost with canned music.
   c. Office expenses—Keep it simple but efficient.
7. Minimize costs within the facilities
   a. Buy previously owned FFEs.
8. Minimize costs within occupancy
   a. Buying land and building increases assets.
   b. Making sure you have adequate insurance coverage against losses.
9. Answers will vary, but may include cooking equipment (pots and pans) and dishes.
10. Answers will vary, but may include in-house or outsourced customer forecasting, accountant, or lawyer.
11. Answers will vary, but may include upgrading of equipment and facilities.
12. Answers will vary, but may include some utilities and retrofit of the building.
13. Answers will vary.
14. Answers will vary.
15. Franchisee must pay the franchisor for the right to sell their product.
16. Controlled expenses can include linens, flatware, decorations, cleaning supplies, certain utilities, menus, product testing, outsourced services, marketing, music, FFE, and landscaping. Proper training and oversight of employees can help control these costs.

ANSWERS TO WORKBOOK PROBLEMS

4. Laundry, maintenance, cleaning, computers, parking, advertising
6. Maintenance, depreciation, insurance, not your expertise
7. Train employees, use cheaper towels, use better towels, use cloth towels
8. Often cheaper to maintain than to repair

13

The Menu as a Marketing Tool

CHAPTER OBJECTIVES

After finishing this chapter the students will be able to:

- Evaluate a menu as a marketing tool
- Evaluate menu design techniques and principles, including:
  - Physical menu characteristics
  - Focal point
  - Methods of emphasis
  - Menu diversity
  - Signature dish
  - Menu layout
  - Menu descriptions
- Perform a menu analysis
- Analyze data from a menu analysis

ANSWERS TO TEXT PROBLEMS

1. It sells the product to the customer.
2. Advantages: Price changes are easy, increased turnover, limited variety in the kitchen
   Disadvantages: Possible food waste, higher menu prices, guest feels less in charge
3. Advantages: Possible check average increase, customer choice
   Disadvantages: Extra purchasing and preparation, added controls needed
4. One-page menu: Just below the centerline of the menu
   Two-page menu: Top of the diagonal line on the second page from top left corner to bottom right corner
5. The most profitable item (the one with the highest contribution item)
6. a. Popular/unprofitable: Change recipe or sales price.
   b. Popular/profitable: Leave it alone.
   c. Unpopular/profitable: Market the item.
   d. Unpopular/profitable: Market the item.
   e. Popular/unprofitable: Change recipe or sales price.
7. a. Unpopular/unprofitable: This item does not sell well and when it does, it does not generate a big profit.
   b. Unpopular/profitable: This item does not sell well but when it does, it does generate a big profit.
   c. Popular/unprofitable: This item sells well but does not generate a big profit.
   d. Popular/profitable: This item sells well and does generate a big profit.

8. a. Unpopular/unprofitable: Take off the menu.
   b. Unpopular/profitable: Move it on the menu.
   c. Popular/unprofitable: Raise price slowly.
   d. Popular/profitable: Leave it alone.
9. If it is too small and hard to read, patrons won't order it. Large font draws attention.
10. Menu diversity is needed for the restaurant operation because it will attract a variety of customers. Large groups will find something for everyone in their party.
11. A signature dish is any product that is unique to an establishment and cannot be, or is not, recreated elsewhere. It allows the restaurant to price it at what the market will bear and can draw loyal customer following.
12. Answers will vary.
13. Answers will vary.
14. Font size, bold font, place on menu, focal point
15. a. Help to protect consumers from fraudulent food and beverage claims.
    b. Point of origin of the product advertised affects quality of the product.
    c. Quantities are correctly stated.
16. a. Unpopular/unprofitable: Take off the menu.
    b. Popular/profitable: Leave it alone.
    c. Popular/profitable: Leave it alone.
    d. Unpopular/unprofitable: Remove from the menu.
    e. Popular/unprofitable: Raise price slowly.
    f. Popular/unprofitable: Raise price slowly.
17. a. Popular/profitable: Leave it alone.
    b. Popular/profitable: Leave it alone.
    c. Unpopular/unprofitable: Remove from the menu.
    d. Popular/unprofitable: Raise price slowly.

ANSWERS TO WORKBOOK PROBLEMS

1. Design, suggestive
2. Guest in mind
3. Faction of potential customers
4. Items you want to sell frequently, profitable items, items that contribute to the CM

5.

Entrée class	Price/sale	Number sold	Total sales	Popularity ratio	Is this entrée profitable?
Steak	$20.00	120	**$2,400**	**.39**	**Yes**
Seafood	$18.00	63	**$1,134**	**.19**	**Yes**
Chicken	$12.00	108	**$1,296**	**.21**	**Yes**
Pork	$12.00	18	**$216**	**.04**	**No**
Vegetarian	$9.00	51	**$459**	**.08**	**Yes**
Pasta	$8.00	28	**$224**	**.04**	**No**
Lamb	$23.00	9	**$207**	**.02**	**No**
Roast	$8.00	17	**$136**	**.02**	**No**
TOTAL	X	**414**	**$6,072**	X	X

6. a.

	A Item cost (dollars)	B Sell price	C Number sold	D Total cost	E Total revenue	F Item food cost %	G Amount of profit per item	H Amount of profit for all sales
a.	1.00	**$2.50**	10	**$10.00**	**$25.00**	**40%**	**$1.50**	**$15.00**
b.	1.50	**$3.75**	10	**$15.00**	**$37.50**	**40%**	**$2.25**	**$22.50**
c.	2.00	**$5.00**	25	**$50.00**	**$125.00**	**40%**	**$3.00**	**$75.00**
d.	2.50	**$6.25**	15	**$37.50**	**$93.75**	**40%**	**$3.75**	**$56.25**
e.	2.60	**$6.50**	15	**$39.00**	**$97.50**	**40%**	**$3.90**	**$58.50**
f.	2.85	**$14.25**	20	**$57.00**	**$285.00**	**20%**	**$11.40**	**$228.00**
g.	3.00	**$15.00**	15	**$45.00**	**$225.00**	**20%**	**$12.00**	**$180.00**
h.	3.10	**$15.50**	25	**$77.50**	**$387.50**	**20%**	**$12.40**	**$310.00**
i.	6.00	**$30.00**	10	**$60.00**	**$300.00**	**20%**	**$24.00**	**$240.00**
j.	1.25	**$6.25**	15	**$18.75**	**$93.75**	**20%**	**$5.00**	**$75.00**
				TOTAL COST **$409.75**	TOTAL REVENUE **$670.00**	TOTAL FC% **25%**		TOTAL PROFIT **$1,260.25**

b. Business decisions—others do it—competition

c. See table (a.)

d. "h" best, "a" worst

e. "i" makes the most money per sale, but sales are small

f. $240 – $18.75 = $221.25 more profit

g. Sales in the past are an indicator of the future if nothing else changes

h. Usually doesn't count
i. "f" and "h" good on both counts; "a" and "b" poor on both
j. How would you deal with each? Advertise, promote. Possibly eliminate "a" and "b"

7. A differentiated product is different from the competition
8. A signature item is unique to the establishment and cannot be or is not recreated elsewhere

14

Forecasts in Sales; Controls in Sales and Revenue

CHAPTER OBJECTIVES

After finishing this chapter the students will be able to:

- Understand the steps to forecasting
- Differentiate among qualitative and quantitative data
- Examine POS data
- Calculate a menu analysis
- Explore various sales control techniques
- Explore methods of theft protection

ANSWERS TO TEXT PROBLEMS

1. Answers will vary, but should include that forecasting allows for proper planning in both labor and purchasing expenses. Proper forecasting can lead to better customer satisfaction.
2. 1. Predict the number of customers.
   2. Check surroundings.
   3. Establish total expected sales.
   4. Use popularity index (menu mix).
   5. Prepare production schedule.
   6. Monitor/reconcile (correct for the future).
3. Quantitative data is based on historical calculations and is actual and verifiable. Qualitative data is less precise, and is based on quality issues that allow for interpretation. These may include weather conditions, traffic issues, and other external factors.
4. It is a computer that can maintain records, print food and drink orders, print checks, and calculate sales figures.
5. A point of sale (POS) system can assist in proper forecasting, and help establish purchasing quantities and labor schedules.
6. It helps figure out how many of each dish should be prepared once total sales forecasts are made.
7. Menu mix can also be used to create a production schedule.
8. Answers may vary, but may include bonded employees, numbered checks, protecting against theft and pilferage.
9. Answers may vary, but may include POS and outsourcing forecasts.

10. Different timelines may be needed because different days of the week produce different sales levels or there may be adjustments for recent increase or decrease in business.
11. Answers will vary, but may include that there is a human element to adjust for qualitative data and forecast irrelevance.
12. When compiling data, management must take into account relevancy of past data. It depends on the situation and clientele.
13. Pros: Increase in sales volume
    Cons: Percentage that is charged by card company, transaction fees
14. Item A: 7.03%
    Item B: 11.93%
    Item C: 23.55%
    Item D: 16.51%
    Item E: 27.83%
    Item F: 13.15%
15. 37
16. Soup A: 12
    Soup B: 29
    Soup C: 21
    Soup D: 17
    Soup E: 15
17. 19 customers

ANSWERS TO WORKBOOK PROBLEMS

1. a. Gives overall numbers to base forecasts on
   b. Gives an overview of the past
   c. Helps tabulate past sales electronically
   d. Defines data that is most likely reliable
   e. Help determine if data is valid for the current time and conditions
2. a. dupe: Copy of a guest check—used to minimize theft
   b. cashier's report: Detailed report on sales and related data
   c. post-service checklist: Determines if policies and procedures complete and followed. A list of checks and balances.
3. House credit, cash, credit cards

4. Answer the questions below given this chart. Dates 1–7 are last week. Dates 8–14 are last year, same week.

	M **1**	**T** **2**	**W** **3**	**T** **4**	**F** **5**	**S** **6**	**S** **7**		**M** **8**	**T** **9**	**W** **10**	**T** **11**	**F** **12**	**S** **13**	**S** **14**
Chicken	20	23	56	55	100	95	12		20	18	20	16	181	210	12
Seafood	21	21	18	19	32	37	7		21	25	18	19	30	35	10
Steak	51	50	51	41	108	121	35		50	50	60	83	120	158	35
Pasta	12	18	12	19	20	28	35		10	18	18	16	12	35	30
Side salads	100	67	121	119	261	26	91		100	121	133	136	280	280	95
Desserts	56	71	71	75	212	201	160		56	71	70	80	216	210	181
Food Totals	**104**	**112**	**137**	**134**	**260**	**281**	**89**		**101**	**111**	**116**	**134**	**343**	**438**	**87**

Based on the preceding chart:

	Friday	Saturday
Chicken	32.3%	32.3%
Seafood	13.9%	12.98%
Steak	40.9%	41.8%
Pasta	12.9%	12.9%

	Mon.	Tues.	Wed.	Thurs.
Chicken	16	16	30	28
Seafood	18	18	14	15
Steak	40	40	44	50
Pasta	9	14	12	14
Side salad	80	75	102	102
Dessert	45	57	56	62

15

Maximizing Sales

CHAPTER OBJECTIVES

After finishing this chapter the students will be able to:

- Differentiate among menu designs
- Calculate menu prices using a variety of methods
- Evaluate the importance of a signature dish
- Evaluate techniques to improve sales
- Implement different suggestive selling techniques and correlate the value of effective suggestive selling
- Distinguish the components of a pre-shift meeting
- Investigate employee empowerment

ANSWERS TO TEXT PROBLEMS

1. Answers will vary, but may include number of guests, sections, specials, suggestive or selling techniques.
2. It gives the employee the drive to interact more effectively with customers, increasing the level of customer service.
3. Answers will vary, but may include comping a meal, sending a drink, moving a guest room, or upgrading a room.
4. Adding an additional course, promoting something that has higher contribution margin
5. The guest, the server, and the owner. The guest has a better experience, the server makes a larger tip, and the owner generates more profit.
6. Items that have a high contribution margin
7. Answers will vary, but may include font size, focal point, bold type, and pictures that will entice the guest to order the item.
8. "Follow the leader pricing," individual price method, actual cost method, and contribution margin method.
9. It differentiates the establishment.
10. $10.21
11. Answers will vary.
12. Food cost: $0.18
    Selling price: $0.86

ANSWERS TO WORKBOOK PROBLEMS

1. a.
   b. Sales price: $7.50
   c.
   d.

	If sales $6.25	If sales $7.50	If sales $0.00
Fixed labor	**$2**	**$200**	**$200**
Other labor	**$70**	**$100**	
Food	**$236**	**$262**	
Other	**$101**	**$113**	
Profit / Loss	**$68**	**$112**	

2. Using the actual cost method complete:

	Cost	Selling Price at 20% F.C.	At 30% F.C.
Dessert #1	$1.25	**$6.25**	**$4.17**
Dessert #2	$1.63	**$8.15**	**$5.43**
Dessert #3	$2.15	**$10.75**	**$7.17**
Dessert #4	$2.25	**$11.25**	**$7.50**
Dessert #5	$3.10	**$15.50**	**$10.33**

3. Advertise, specials, signature items, cheaper prices
4. a. cooks: Garnishes, new staff, speed, unhappy customers, and train staff preparation
   b. servers: Speed, new staff, promotions, cleanliness, and new menu items

Answers to the Student Workbook Final Exam Prep

1. a. 30%
   b. 24.6%
   c. 34%
   d. 6%
   e. 35%
   f. 26%
   g. 7.20%
   h. $7,837
   i. $1,780
   j. $9,618
   k. $2,368
   l. 30%
   m. $3,393
   n. 7.2%
   o. $2,693
2. Increase of $4,003 per day
3.

	a	b	c	d	e
Menu item	**Sales**	**Sales % of total sales**	**Cost**	**CF % of each category cost/sales d = c / a**	**CF % of each category cost/total sales e = c/a (total)**
Entrees	$1,677,440	59%	$570,330	**34%**	20%
Appetizers	$513,232	**18%**	$46,191	9%	**1.6%**
Desserts	$418,608	**15%**	$58,605	**14%**	2.1%
Non-alcoholic beverages	$212,120	**8%**	$12,727	6%	**.05%**
TOTALS	**$2,821,400**	xxxxxxxxxx	**$852,639**	xxxxxxxxxx	xxxxxxxxx

4. beverages—low cost %
5. a. $966,813 up from $252,062
   b. $1,936,285 up from $1,221,534
   c. ($246,744) down from $468,007
   d. 55.9%
6. a. Fixed costs: $961,377
   b. CM (Contribution Margin): $1,429,384
   c. CR (Contribution Rate): .41
   d. VR (Variable Rate): .59
7.

	On-hand amount	Par amount	Safety factor amount	Total amount to order
Entrees	300	500	**50**	**250**
Appetizers	135	300	**30**	**195**
Desserts	216	300	**30**	**114**
Non-alcoholic beverages	280	600	**60**	**380**

8. 55.5 lbs. and $444
9. Yes, $.25 per steak cheaper
   a.

Menu item	Total sold	Average check per item
Entrees	67,097	**$24.85**
Appetizers	34,215	**$15.00**
Desserts	59,801	**$7.00**
Non-alcoholic beverages	106,060	**$2.00**

10.

	AUG	SEPT	OCT	NOV	DEC	JAN
OI	$16,200	$17,100	$17,250	$18,000	$14,320	$14,000
CI	$17,100	$17,350	$18,000	$14,320	$14,000	$14,200
P	$68,200	$71,100	$70,100	$72,200	$68,100	$62,300
CF	**$67,300**	**$70,850**	**$69,350**	**$75,880**	**$68,320**	**$62,100**
AI	**$16,500**	**$17,225**	**$17,625**	**$16.160**	**$14,160**	**$14,100**
IT	**4.04**	**4.11**	**3.93**	**4.7**	**4.82**	**4.4**
	FEB	**MAR**	**APRIL**	**MAY**	**JUNE**	**JULY**
OI	$14,200	$16,100	$16,200	$17,200	$17,300	$17,300
CI	$16,100	$16,200	$17,200	$17,300	$17,300	$16,200
P	$65,000	$61,000	$67,200	$67,440	$99,999	$80,000
CF	**$63,100**	**$60,900**	**$66,200**	**$67,340**	**$99,999**	**$81,100**
AI	**$15,150**	**$16,150**	**$16,700**	**$17,250**	**$17,300**	**$16,750**
IT	**4.17**	**3.77**	**3.96**	**3.9**	**5.78**	**4.84**

11.

Item	Size in ounces	Cost per item	Number sold	Total item cost	Total item sales	Profit
Appetizer A	8	$2.00	10	**$20.00**	**$133.33**	**$113.33**
Appetizer B	8	$2.50	15	**$37.5**	**$250.00**	**$212.50**
Appetizer C	6	$2.00	15	**$30.00**	**$200.00**	**$170.00**
Appetizer D	6	$3.00	20	**$60.00**	**$400.00**	**$360.00**
Steak A	12	$4.00	5	**$20.00**	**$80.00**	**$60.00**
Steak B	12	$4.00	32	**$128.00**	**$512.00**	**$384.00**
Steak C	10	$5.00	60	**$300.00**	**$1,200.00**	**$900.00**
Steak D	8	$6.00	25	**$150.00**	**$600.00**	**$450.00**
Seafood A	6	$3.00	23	**$69.00**	**$460.00**	**$391.00**
Seafood B	6	$4.00	40	**$160.00**	**$1,060.66**	**$900.66**
Seafood C	8	$5.00	12	**$60.00**	**$400.00**	**$340.00**
Seafood D	8	$4.00	12	**$48.00**	**$320.00**	**$372.00**
Poultry A	8	$3.00	28	**$84.00**	**$560.00**	**$476.00**
Poultry B	8	$3.00	25	**$75.00**	**$500.00**	**$425.00**
Poultry C	6	$5.00	25	**$75.00**	**$500.00**	**$425.00**
Poultry D	8	$3.00	25	**$75.00**	**$500.00**	**$425.00**
Beverage A	10	$.50	90	**$45.00**	**$64.28**	**$19.28**
Beverage B	12	$.50	89	**$44.50**	**$63.57**	**$22.07**
Beverage C	14	$.50	121	**$60.50**	**$86.43**	**$25.93**
Beverage D	12	$.50	154	**$77.00**	**$110.00**	**$33.00**
Dessert A	8	$1.00	32	**$32.00**	**$213.33**	**$181.33**
Dessert B	8	$1.00	78	**$78.00**	**$520.00**	**$172.00**
Dessert C	8	$2.00	65	**$130.00**	**$866.60**	**$736.66**
Dessert D	8	$2.00	34	**$68.00**	**$453.33**	**$385.33**

c. What items produced the most profit? Why? Steak C, Seafood B, Dessert C

d. Which items were the most popular? Why? Steak C, Seafood B
Dessert B and C
Beverage A, B, C, and D

e. Which items would you promote more? Why? Appetizer A; Steak A, B, D; Seafood C and D
High sales, high profit

f. Which items might you remove from the menu? Why? Steak A

g. Which items might you consider raising the price? Why? Steak B, C, Seafood B, all beverages, Desserts B, C
h. What items would you promote to raise the average check if everyone already orders an entrée? All desserts

12.

	Number of people	Hours worked this week	Average pay rate	Benefits	Total pay
Management	3	185	$1,800/wk.	35%	**$7,290**
Cooks	12	480	$12/hr.	30%	**$7,488**
Servers	14	420	$3/hr.	30%	**$1,638**
Dishwashers	6	240	$8/hr.	30%	**$2,496**
Busers	6	200	$6/hr.	30%	**$1,560**
Administrative	1	40	$8/hr.	30%	**$416**
Chef	1	62	$1,700/wk.	35%	**$2,295**

a. Total payroll? $23,183
b. If benefits for the chef go up to 40%. +$850, new payroll total is $24,033
c. What are the total turnover costs? $801
d. What is the new cooks' total pay? Less $288
e. What is the cost of labor %? 28.98%

13. You would save by outsourcing, because you now pay $8/hour and $2.40/hour in benefits.
    a. Quality of work and dependability of workers.
14. a. purchase software programs
    b. scheduling software that can schedule and analyze variances
    c. software that can analyze food cost and labor cost variances
    d. software that can analyze best sellers, profits, and times items sell best
    e. written job descriptions as well as written questions and tests to help evaluate the best hire prospects
18. a. $8,526.39
    b. $4,380.00
    c. $12,906.39
19. If conditions such as the weather remained the same, you could forecast similar sales a year later. Promotions could increase sales.

20.

		"A"			"B"	
		New	**% of sales**		**New**	**% of sales**
Check average	$10	**$11**		$10	**$11**	
Number of meals sold	400	**380**		1,000	**950**	
Income / meal	$4,000	**$4,180**		$10,000	**$10,450**	
Fixed costs	$1,000	**$1,000**		$1,000	**$1,000**	
Variable costs	$800	**$836**	**20%**	$1,600	**$1,672**	**16%**
Food costs	$1,400	**$1,463**	**35%**	$3,500	**$3,657**	**35%**
Labor costs	$1,400	**$1,463**	**35%**	$3,000	**$3,135**	**30%**
Profit	($600)	**$(582)**		$900	**$986**	

21. Brand A is the best buy.

22.

Month	2005 sales	Predicted increase for next year	Increase amount	Total 2006 projected sales amount
Jan	$12,000	7%	**$840**	**$12,840**
Feb	14,000	7%	**980**	**14,980**
Mar	14,000	8%	**1,120**	**15,120**
Apr	16,000	7.5%	**1,200**	**17,200**
May	22,000	4%	**880**	**22,880**
June	19,000	4%	**760**	**19,760**
Total	**$97,000**	XXXXXXX	**$5,780**	**$102,780**

Test Bank

CHAPTER 1

True/False

1. The purpose of cost control is to manage labor and inventory in order to ensure profitability for an organization.
2. Management's role in the control process includes planning, organizing, directing, and controlling.
3. Overhead costs are costs associated with food, beverage, and labor.
4. Fixed costs are usually non-controllable, while variable costs are usually controllable.
5. Average costs are what management expects the costs to be in the future.
6. Depreciation is a deductible allowance given to the manager of a restaurant.

Multiple Choice

1. Variable costs do not include:
   a. food costs.
   b. beverage costs.
   c. salaried employees.
   d. non-salaried employees.
2. Which of the following is considered a semi-variable expense?
   a. Labor cost
   b. Food cost
   c. Beverage cost
   d. Actual cost
3. The percentage of sales for any item within a certain category is called:
   a. sales by category.
   b. average sales.
   c. total sales.
   d. sales mix.
4. Food cost percent is calculated by using which of the following formulas?
   a. Food Cost × Food Sales
   b. Labor Cost / Total Sales
   c. Food Cost / Food Sales
   d. Food Sales / Food Cost

5. If sales are $1,023.50 and costs are $275.22, food cost percent is:
   a. 21.19%.
   b. 26.89%.
   c. 37.19%.
   d. 73.12%.

Short Answer

1. Calculate the sales mix for the week at Patty's Burger Shack with the following sales numbers:

   Hamburger—237
   Cheeseburger—412
   Double cheeseburger—503
   Chicken burger—177
   Fish burger—81

2. List three examples of fixed costs in the foodservice industry.
3. List three examples of variable costs in the foodservice industry.

CHAPTER 2

True/False

1. Cost of goods issued reflects the cost of foods that are no longer in the storeroom.
2. Transfers-in are the costs associated with food or beverage that has been charged to a kitchen and then sent to another outlet.
3. Employee meals offered in an establishment generate sales.
4. When calculating cost of food sold, items that generate sales are deducted from the cost of food issued, and items that do not generate sales are added to the cost of food issued.
5. An operating budget is prepared prior to the start of the period it is written for.
6. A restaurant has a choice of purchasing 10 pounds of strawberry jam for $12.95, or making their own strawberry jam. The ingredients for making 10 pounds of strawberry jam include 5 pounds of strawberries and 5 pounds of sugar. If strawberries are $2.12 a pound and sugar is $8.46 for 20 pounds, the restaurant should make its own strawberry jam.

Multiple Choice

1. The manager of Cup of Jo's Coffee Shop has established that it will serve freshly brewed Folger's coffee to its customers. This is an example of a:
   a. quality standard.
   b. quantity standard.
   c. cost/price standard.
   d. None of the above
2. Sidewalk Chalk Café's famous BLT sandwich is made with two slices of sourdough bread, four strips of bacon, five slices of lettuce, and three slices of tomatoes. This is an example of a:
   a. quality standard.
   b. quantity standard.
   c. cost/price standard.
   d. None of the above
3. Last month's ending food inventory was $37,487. This month's ending food inventory is $39,860. Food purchases this month were $69,500. Food worth $725 and liquor worth $862 was transferred from the bar to the kitchen. Employee meals totaled $1,133. The cost of food sold equals:
   a. $65,857.
   b. $66,131.
   c. $70,603.
   d. $70,877.
4. This tool is often used in the restaurant industry when deciding whether or not it is cost effective to make something on the premises or use a convenient pre-prepared product.
   a. Standard operating procedures
   b. Operating budget
   c. Profit and loss statement
   d. Make or buy analysis

5. Outsourcing has become popular in the hospitality industry due to the:
   a. potential savings that can be attained.
   b. brand recognition that will draw additional customers into an operation.
   c. expertise of outside companies.
   d. All the above

Short Answer

1. Why is it important to establish standards in the hospitality industry?
2. Explain quality standard, and give some examples.
3. Explain quantity standard, and give some examples.
4. Explain cost/price standard, and give some examples.
5. A restaurant with 150 seats will be open for lunch Monday through Saturday, and for dinner only on Friday. Seat turnover for lunch is estimated to be 2.1, with dinner turnover at 1.8. The average food check for lunch is expected to be $7.85, with a dinner average food check of $12.36. Beverage revenue is estimated at 17% of lunch food sales, plus 23% of dinner food sales. Food cost is expected to be 27% of total food sales, and beverage cost is expected to be 15% of total beverage sales. Salaried employees are estimated at 8% of total sales, with wages for all other employees forecasted to be 20% of total sales. Benefits are expected to be an additional 16% of total salaries and wages. Other controllable expenses are estimated at 6% of total revenue. Depreciation is expected to be $12,000 per year, with occupancy costs and interest charges of $26,893 and $7,341 per year, respectively. Create a yearly operating budget.

CHAPTER 3

True/False

25 1. The four main reasons behind constant new technology in the hospitality industry are to ensure guest comfort and enjoyment, control costs, generate increased sales and control of revenue, and make employee jobs easier.

26 2. Data mining provides information to operators about consumers by extracting hidden facts within databases.

27 3. A hotel that utilizes check-in and check-out kiosks eliminates the need for guests to stand in line for a transaction. This decreases employee numbers and labor costs, as well as customer satisfaction and customer service.

28 4. Technology has become a tool for restaurants to increase their reach in clientele, effectively advertise their restaurant at low costs, and can aid in handling increasing sales volume.

Multiple Choice

29 1. Technology advances create opportunities for a business in the hospitality industry to realize:
   a. guest satisfaction.
   b. financial savings.
   c. service quality.
   d. marketing success.

30 2. This program can be implemented by any property to control costs:
   a. Inventory control system
   b. Temperature control system
   c. Data mining
   d. Guest check-in and check-out kiosks

31 3. This system can efficiently help increase security and accountability in control of revenue:
   a. Cash register
   b. Video surveillance
   c. Manager assistance
   d. Point of sales

32 4. The four main goals that drive technology are:
   a. guest comfort, control costs, increase sales and control revenue, and labor costs savings.
   b. control equipment costs, control labor costs, control revenue, and control food costs.
   c. guest comfort, control costs, decrease sales and control revenue, and labor costs.
   d. control labor costs, control energy costs, control revenue, and control sales.

33 5. Data mining provides information about:
   a. previous employees.
   b. sales.
   c. customers.
   d. inventory.

6. Although technology is available to all companies, it is not widely utilized by small companies because:
    a. of installation complications.
    b. training requires too much time.
    c. the company has no use for it.
    d. equipment is expensive.
7. The advantage of having check-in and check-out kiosks in hotel lobbies is that they:
    a. speed and simplify the process for guests.
    b. decrease employee numbers and labor costs.
    c. increase guest satisfaction and customer service.
    d. All of the above
8. Through the use of these, guests have access to the hotel room, other hotel services, charging retail items, meals, and other purchases:
    a. Magnetic key card
    b. Smart cards
    c. Point of sales systems
    d. Kiosks

Short Answer

1. Describe three types of packaging techniques used in the food and beverage industry.
2. How does a combination oven save money?

CHAPTER 4

True/False

1. Variable costs change with the increase or decrease in the volume of business, and are expressed as dollar figures that represent the actual cost of a product or service that is for sale.
2. Contribution rate is defined as the fixed costs and the profit generated by sales.
3. Variable rate is the percentage of sales that goes toward paying for the variable costs.
4. Contribution rate is the percentage of sales that goes towards paying for the fixed costs and generating profit.
5. Contribution rate is defined as 1 – variable costs.
6. The break-even point is the point at which a business is self-sufficient and pays all of its bills, but does not generate profit.
7. If fixed costs are $100,000, and the contribution rate is 65%, then sales must be $153,846.15 to break even.

Multiple Choice

1. All of the following are correct equations except:
   a. sales = variable costs + fixed costs + profit.
   b. sales = variable costs + contribution margin.
   c. variable costs = sales – fixed costs + profit.
   d. fixed costs = sales – variable costs – profit.
2. If sales are $250,000, variable costs are $75,000, and fixed costs are $120,000, profit is:
   a. $45,000.
   b. $55,000.
   c. $205,000.
   d. $250,000.
3. If variable costs are $17,000, contribution margin is $58,000, and profit is $11,500, sales are:
   a. $28,500.
   b. $63,500.
   c. $75,000.
   d. $86,500.
4. If sales are $310,000, variable costs are $120,000, and fixed costs are $173,000, the contribution margin is:
   a. $17,000.
   b. $190,000.
   c. $257,000.
   d. $293,000.
5. If sales are $125,000, and variable costs are $62,000, the variable rate is:
   a. 20.16%.
   b. 49.60%.
   c. 50.40%.
   d. 79.84%.

48

6. If fixed costs are $15,000, profit is $9,000, and contribution rate is 37.25%, then sales are:
   a. $8,940.00.
   b. $9,561.75.
   c. $16,107.38.
   d. $64,429.53.

49

7. If sales are $200,000, and variable costs are $75,000, the contribution rate is:
   a. 37.50%.
   b. 45.50%.
   c. 62.50%.
   d. 73.50%.

8. If fixed costs are $175,000 and the variable rate is 35%, and management has decided that they want to generate a profit of $45,000, how much sales will be needed?
   a. $269,230.77
   b. $338,461.54
   c. $500,000.00
   d. $628,571.43

9. If fixed costs are $65,000, average sales price is $17.45, and variable rate is 0.32, the break-even point in unit sales is:
   a. 2,533.
   b. 3,725.
   c. 5,476.
   d. 11,641.

Short Answer

50

1. Describe three ways to change the break-even point.
2. Calculate average variable rate, average contribution margin, and the average check for the following menu items:

Item	Cost	Number sold	Selling price
Cheese pizza	$3.00	45	$11.99
Pepperoni pizza	$3.27	60	$14.99
Hawaiian pizza	$3.75	23	$15.99
Sausage pizza	$4.00	52	$14.99
BBQ Chicken pizza	$4.25	65	$17.99

CHAPTER 5

True/False

1. A purchase specification is a listing of all the criteria for ingredients and supplies, including information such as grade, color, size, and place of origin.
2. A minimum safety stock is created so that when the inventory reaches this low level, it triggers the buyer to purchase additional product.
3. In the physical inventory method, all products are physically counted and valued.
4. If the perpetual inventory method is used in an establishment, it is not necessary to take a physical inventory count.
5. A recipe for mashed potatoes requires 5 pounds of peeled potatoes. This means that 5 pounds of potatoes is the as purchased (AP) amount needed.

Multiple Choice

1. Kiki's Snack Corner uses this type of ordering method, in which the quantity of product ordered remains the same, while the order dates change, fluctuating around the needs of the restaurant.
   a. Periodic ordering method
   b. Perpetual ordering method
   c. Standard ordering method
   d. None of the above
2. Denny's Diner uses this type of ordering method, in which the order dates are set at consistent intervals, and order quantities change according to the needed amount.
   a. Periodic ordering method
   b. Perpetual ordering method
   c. Standard ordering method
   d. None of the above
3. Uncle Rico's Taco Shop uses the periodic order method for ordering flour tortillas weekly. On average, Uncle Rico's Taco Shop uses five cases (10 packs per case) of flour tortillas per week. Currently, there are five packs on hand. If the desired ending inventory is 10 packs, how many cases of flour tortillas need to be ordered today?
   a. 4
   b. 5
   c. 6
   d. 7
4. Pete's Pizzeria uses the perpetual order method for ordering canned tomato sauce. Normally, the restaurant uses 12 cans per day. The par stock is six cases of tomato sauce (16 cans per case), and the safety stock is 25%. If it takes four days to receive a delivery of tomato sauce, how many cases of tomato sauce need to be reordered?
   a. 3
   b. 5
   c. 6
   d. 8

5. This form of purchasing allows small operations to combine their purchasing needs with other small operations so that items can be purchased in larger quantities, and then split up among the many buyers.
   a. Cost plus purchasing
   b. Co-operative purchasing
   c. One-stop shopping
   d. Centralized purchasing
6. This form of purchasing is becoming the fastest-growing segment of all buying plans because of its accessibility and affordability.
   a. Open bid purchasing
   b. Seal bid purchasing
   c. Warehouse buying
   d. On-line purchasing
7. If zucchini has a yield percent of 65, how much needs to be purchased to have an edible portion of 12.5 pounds?
   a. 8 lbs. 2 oz.
   b. 9 lbs. 4 oz.
   c. 19 lbs. 4 oz.
   d. 35 lbs. 11 oz.
8. If you have 8 pounds of mushrooms, with a loss percent of 53, how much edible product will be left?
   a. 3 lbs. 12 oz.
   b. 4 lbs. 4 oz.
   c. 15 lbs. 2 oz.
   d. 17 lbs. 1 oz.
9. 20 pounds of carrots were purchased at $0.50 per pound. After preparation, there are 17 pounds left. The edible portion cost per pound is:
   a. $0.42.
   b. $0.43.
   c. $0.59.
   d. $1.70.

Short Answer

1. Explain the difference between open bid purchasing and seal bid purchasing.

CHAPTER 6

True/False

1. When receiving goods, it is only important to check that the quality and quantity of the products meet the standards set by the establishment.
2. Storage standards include the protection of the product's quality, protection from theft, and accessibility of the product.
3. The safest way to control inventory in a restaurant is to have the person in charge of purchasing also be in charge of receiving, storing, and issuing goods.
4. Directs are products that go directly to the department that utilizes them, bypassing the storeroom both physically and in accounting.
5. Stores are products that get put into the warehouse and are distributed as needed.
6. To ensure accuracy when calculating values of inventory, an establishment should alternate using different methods from period to period.

Multiple Choice

1. All of the following are acceptable means of controlling inventory except:
   a. hiring trustworthy employees.
   b. limiting access to storeroom facilities.
   c. having warehouses located near a parking garage.
   d. using warehouse requisition forms.
2. The most accurate method of valuing inventory is:
   a. first in first out (FIFO).
   b. weighted average inventory.
   c. actual price.
   d. last price.
3. This method of valuing inventory requires labeling each individual item with the price paid and the date on which the item was received:
   a. First in first out (FIFO)
   b. Last in first out (LIFO)
   c. Actual price
   d. Last price
4. This method of valuing inventory values the remaining products at the end of the period using the latest purchase prices.
   a. First in first out (FIFO)
   b. Last in first out (LIFO)
   c. Weighted average inventory
   d. Last price
5. This method of valuing inventory values the remaining products using the first prices paid for the products.
   a. First in first out (FIFO)
   b. Last in first out (LIFO)
   c. Weighted average inventory
   d. Actual price

6. If a restaurant has an opening inventory of $17,523, a closing inventory of $13,777, and purchases of $275,000, the inventory turnover is:
   a. 9.79.
   b. 8.91.
   c. 17.81.
   d. 19.57.

Short Answer

1. Explain the importance of checking quality, quantity, and cost standards during receiving, and how receivers can check for these standards.
2. Calculate the ending inventory value and the cost of food issued for each of the five inventory methods (FIFO, LIFO, Actual, Latest Purchase Price, and Weighted Price), assuming that there are 10 cans left at the end of the month and the following purchases are made:

   12 cans @ $5.35 each
   7 cans @ $5.82 each
   10 cans @ $5.50 each
   15 cans @ $5.10 each
   6 cans @ $5.90 each

3. Inventory turnover is used as a check on the purchasing department. However, management must investigate if the inventory turnover is higher or lower than industry standards or the standards set by the operation. What are the effects of having a high or low inventory turnover?

CHAPTER 7

True/False

1. A standardized recipe should be understandable so that anyone who follows the recipe will be successful in producing the same product with the same taste.
2. A recipe costing sheet details the cost of all the ingredients in a standardized recipe.
3. The standard portion cost is calculated by dividing the total number of portions by the cost of the item.

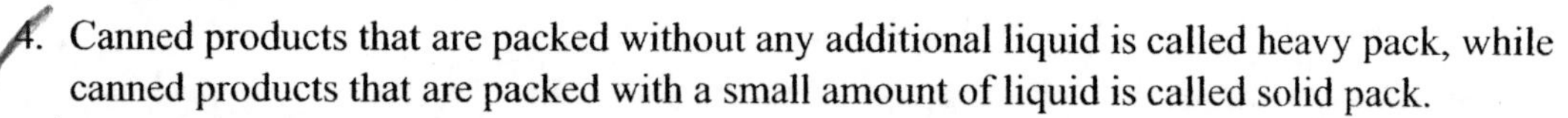

4. Canned products that are packed without any additional liquid is called heavy pack, while canned products that are packed with a small amount of liquid is called solid pack.

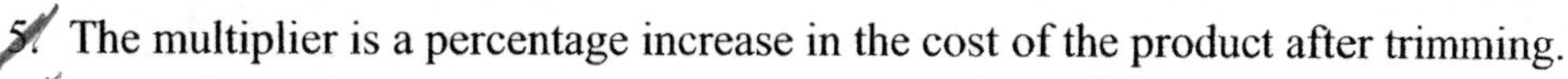

5. The multiplier is a percentage increase in the cost of the product after trimming.
6. To accurately calculate how much meat costs, it is necessary to calculate either a butcher's yield test or a cooking loss test, not both.

Multiple Choice

1. The standard portion size of a hamburger at Bill's Grill is 12 oz. Which standard of measurement is Bill's Grill using for their hamburgers?
   a. Volume
   b. Count
   c. Weight
   d. None of the above
2. A standardized recipe costs $43.00 to produce, and yields 15 portions. The standard cost of one standard portion is:
   a. $0.35.
   b. $1.43.
   c. $2.86.
   d. $2.87.
3. A 30-lb. bag of potatoes, used to make mashed potatoes, costs $25.00. If the standard portion size is 6 oz., the standard portion cost is:
   a. $0.10.
   b. $0.31.
   c. $0.83.
   d. $1.22.
4. The tool used to find out the actual costs associated with buying larger cuts of meat and fabricating it into smaller ready to use cuts is:
   a. recipe costing sheet.
   b. butcher's yield test.
   c. cooking loss test.
   d. food cost to date.
5. The multiplier per pound is calculated using which of the following formulas?
   a. EP cost / AP cost
   b. AP cost / EP cost
   c. EP cost × AP cost
   d. AP cost – EP cost

Short Answer

1. What are some of the causes of under production in a kitchen, and what can be done to prevent it?
2. List the factors that need to be taken into consideration before deciding to purchase a large cut of meat and butchering it in-house.
3. Explain the total cost approach.
4. Using the following information, calculate the food cost and food cost percent for each day and for food cost to date. Use the chart below.

Date	Directs	Stores	Transfers In	Transfers Out	Sales
2/5	$275	$790	$150	$35	$3,422
2/6	$150	$538	$75	$58	$4,310
2/7	$81	$300	$17	$77	$3,709

Date	Food Cost Today	Food Cost to Date	Food Cost % Today	Food Cost % to Date	Food Sales Today	Food Sales to Date
2/5						
2/6						
2/7						

5. Using the following information, complete the butcher's yield test and the cooking loss test. Two ribs of beef, U.S. choice grade, weighing a total of 57 lb. 8 oz., were purchased at $6.39 per pound.

	Breakdown	**Value/lb.**
Fat	8 lb. 6 oz.	$0.10
Bones	5 lb.	$0.45
Short ribs	4 lb. 4 oz.	$3.12
Ground beef	3 lb. 12 oz.	$1.19
Oven-ready prime rib	35 lb. 12 oz.	
Bones and trim	2 lb.	
Cooked weight	33 lb. 8 oz.	

Butcher's Yield

Item: Grade:

Weight

Total Cost: AP Cost

	Weight		Ratio to Value			EP Cost	Multiplier
Breakdown	Lb.	Oz.	Total Lb.	Per Lb.	Total Value	Lb./Oz.	Lb./Oz.
Fat							
Bones							
Short ribs							
Ground beef							
Loss in cutting							
Prime rib							
Total							

Cooking Loss

	Weight		Ratio to Value			EP Cost	Multiplier
Breakdown	Lb.	Oz.	Total Lb.	Per Lb.	Total Value	Lb./Oz.	Lb./Oz.
Original weight							
Trimmed weight							
Loss in trimming							
Cooked weight							
Loss in cooking							
Bones and trim							
Saleable weight							

6. Use the information in problem 5 to answer the following questions.
    a. How many 12 oz. portions will this product yield?
    b. How much beef needs to be purchased to serve 200 portions?
    c. What is the EP cost per serving?
    d. What would the new EP cost per serving be if the AP price changed to $6.73 per pound?

CHAPTER 8

True/False

1. In a licensed state, taxes need to be paid by both the distributor and the end user.
2. All wines, regardless of when or where the grapes are harvested, can contain a vintage.
3. The term *proof* originated through a simple test of pouring liquor over a little gunpowder. If the liquor had adequate alcohol content, it burned with a steady blue flame and eventually ignited the gunpowder.
4. Unlike with food, quality, quantity, and cost standards are not applied when purchasing and receiving beverages.
5. An advantage to purchasing alcoholic beverages is the ability to purchase broken cases of alcohol.
6. Restaurants should always purchase non-alcoholic beverages in the largest size container because it is usually the most cost efficient.
7. An exclusivity clause mandates that an operation can only sell a particular brand.

Multiple Choice

1. This type of state has strict controls over the distribution of alcohol, and permits only state-run stores to sell alcohol.
    a. Licensed
    b. Control
    c. Franchise
    d. Dry
2. This type of state establishes procedures that allow only one distributor to sell a certain brand's product.
    a. Licensed
    b. Control
    c. Franchise
    d. Dry
3. The most cost-effective method of purchasing alcohol is in what size bottle?
    a. 750 milliliter
    b. 1 liter
    c. 1.75 liter
    d. 2 liter
4. Chubby's Bar has an opening storeroom inventory of $56,888, purchases of $350,000, closing storeroom inventory of $73,493, opening bar inventory of $12,000, and closing bar inventory of $9,038. Beverage cost for Chubby's Bar is:
    a. $336,357.
    b. $363,643.
    c. $459,343.
    d. $477,419.

5. If a restaurant has a bar opening inventory of $12,320, a bar closing inventory of $8,583, and purchases of $110,000, the inventory turnover rate is:
   a. 1.03.
   b. 5.44.
   c. 10.88.
   d. 12.52.

Short Answer

1. What are some of the advantages of a licensed state, and the disadvantages of a control state?
2. What are the proper storage procedures for beer, wines, and spirits?
3. Describe the two most common practices implemented when establishing issuing standards for alcoholic beverages.

CHAPTER 9

True/False

1. It is common to see bartenders pour drinks from a 1.75 liter bottle in a front bar.
2. A jigger is a two-sided measurer that has a handle and two cups at the end.
3. It is not uncommon for establishments to take a bar inventory on a daily basis.
4. In a state without dramshop laws, a bartender who serves a patron who later hurts someone due to intoxication can be held responsible for the liability due to the accident.
5. Well brands are served when a customer specifies a specific brand of alcohol, while call brands are served when a customer does not specify a brand name.
6. The beverage differential is the additional revenue generated from selling mixed drinks, as compared to an ounce measure of the liquor.
7. The cost approach to monitoring beverage operations is when each bottle of liquor is given a value based on how many drinks it should generate according to the standards established by management.

Multiple Choice

1. At this type of bar, the pouring is usually done behind the scenes.
   a. Front bar
   b. Service bar
   c. Catering bar
   d. Night club bar
2. At this type of bar, the inventory stocked will depend on the clientele.
   a. Front bar
   b. Service bar
   c. Catering bar
   d. Night club bar
3. This method of pouring drinks has the potential for inconsistency in products and in controlling the actual costs of the drinks.
   a. Automated beverage-dispensing machine
   b. Service gun
   c. Jigger
   d. Free pour
4. This method of pouring beverages is controlled from a beverage storage room, where the liquid is pumped through plastic tubing to the bar.
   a. Automated beverage-dispensing machine
   b. Service gun
   c. Jigger
   d. Free pour
5. This approach to monitoring beverage operations requires a daily physical inventory of every bottle. With this, the actual usage in ounces is compared to the ounces sold.
   a. Cost approach
   b. Liquid measure approach
   c. Sales value approach
   d. Standard approach

6. This approach to monitoring beverage operations requires a monthly inventory to determine the value of the inventory, and is calculated using the same method as with food.
    a. Cost approach
    b. Liquid measure approach
    c. Sales value approach
    d. Standard approach

Short Answer

1. Why is it a good idea for management to develop standardized recipes for beverages and utilize them in an operation?
2. Explain how the type of glassware can affect beverage purchasing and production control?
3. List some of the common scams reported in the industry regarding bartender theft.

CHAPTER 10

True/False

1. The turnover rate of employees in the hospitality industry historically runs around 100%.
2. Costs associated with turnover including the cost to find, replace, and train a new employee are usually not enough to affect the profitability of any operation.
3. Direct and indirect compensations are considered current compensation.
4. When scheduling employees, it is not necessary to adhere to the payroll budget as long as the forecasted needs are met.
5. Unemployment rates are directly related to the amount of turnover in the industry.

Multiple Choice

1. Salaried employees are considered:
   a. variable and controllable expenses.
   b. variable and non-controllable expenses.
   c. fixed and controllable expenses.
   d. fixed and non-controllable expenses.
2. Labor turnover rate refers to the ratio between the number of:
   a. applicants interviewed for positions to the number hired.
   b. departing employees to the total number of employees on staff.
   c. applicants to the number of employees on staff.
   d. departing employees to the number of job positions.
3. Which of the following is a key factor in reducing the labor turnover rate in a restaurant?
   a. Increased minimum wage
   b. Labor contracts
   c. Use of part-time employees
   d. Proper training
4. The Fair Labor Standards Act (FLSA) has established that:
   a. overtime is considered over 40 hours in a consecutive 7-day/24-hour period.
   b. all employees are entitled to a 30-minute break for every six hours of work.
   c. part-time employees are not eligible to receive overtime pay.
   d. overtime payments must be equal to one and a half times the paid wage.
5. Stock options and pensions are forms of this type of employee compensation.
   a. Current
   b. Deferred
   c. Direct
   d. Indirect
6. All of the following are ways to reduce labor cost except:
   a. purchasing machines to take the place of employees.
   b. preparing foods at a commissary location.
   c. hiring a full-time employee to transfer foods from the storeroom to the kitchen.
   d. limiting the diversity of a menu.

Short Answer

1. Describe the difference between salaried employees and hourly employees.
2. What are some of the consequences of improper training of employees?
3. What are the advantages of outsourcing?
4. List three forms of employee compensation.

CHAPTER 11

True/False

1. Before an organizational chart can be created, a task analysis needs to be completed.
2. A cost–benefit analysis is used to compare the costs associated with doing a task in-house and the benefit realized if the task is outsourced.
3. If an employee "buys in" to the philosophy and goals of management, he or she is more likely to be successful and happy with his or her job.
4. Productivity is defined as the quality or state of yielding results.
5. Labor cost standards are directly interrelated to food cost standards—the higher the food cost, the higher the labor cost, and the lower the food cost, the lower the labor cost.
6. Job specifications describe where and when specific tasks need to be done.
7. Training new hires as well as current employees is a critical task for management in the hospitality industry.

Multiple Choice

1. This is the result of answering a series of questions related to what needs to be done, when it needs to be done, and how it needs to be done.
   a. Task analysis
   b. Cost–benefit analysis
   c. Job specification
   d. Job description
2. If a restaurant establishes that there will always be one server per three tables on duty, the standard being met is:
   a. quality.
   b. quantity.
   c. cost.
   d. None of the above
3. A formal restaurant establishes that its entire kitchen staff must attend, or have attended culinary school. This is an example of what type of labor standard?
   a. Quality
   b. Quantity
   c. Cost
   d. None of the above
4. Which of the following is example of an effective job description?
   a. Be able to clean a room.
   b. Be able to cook a steak rare, medium-rare, medium, medium-well, and well.
   c. Be able to operate a minimum of four sauté pans simultaneously.
   d. Be able to operate a computer and use an Excel spreadsheet.
5. Using this training method, employees learn the needed skills and standard by watching or working with present employees.
   a. On-the-job training
   b. Distance learning
   c. Off-site training
   d. Cross training

Short Answer

1. What is a job description, and why is it important for an operation to have clearly defined job descriptions?
2. Describe two motivational tools management can use to keep employees happily working in a positive working environment.
3. Describe three monitoring methods used in the hospitality industry.

CHAPTER 12

True/False

1. A marketing budget includes expenses for newspaper advertisements, coupons, and television ads, as well as free meals.
2. Not all businesses and restaurants that play background music in their establishment are required to pay royalties to music organizations.
3. The lifetime cost of a piece of equipment includes the initial purchase price, delivery costs, installation and testing costs, relevant operating costs, repairs, maintenance, and the trade-in value.

Multiple Choice

1. After undergoing new management, Aunt Betty's Bistro has decided to use linens. Aunt Betty's Bistro's next major decision is:
   a. what color linens to use.
   b. to purchase or rent linens.
   c. what kind of chairs to use.
   d. how to rearrange the tables.
2. The costs associated with cleaning supplies can be controlled and maintained at the proper level by:
   a. proper training.
   b. using proper quality cleaning supplies.
   c. reducing cleaning duties.
   d. both a and b
3. Costs associated with ______________ are a large component of the costs of opening a business.
   a. linens
   b. menus
   c. landscape
   d. furniture, fixtures, and equipment

Short Answer

1. Explain franchise fees.
2. List two methods of purchasing that can minimize the costs associated with purchasing equipment.
3. Describe three costs associated with occupancy.

CHAPTER 13

True/False

1. All restaurants should have a target audience; however, most successful restaurants focus on trying to serve a very broad category of customers.
2. The focal point of a menu is the first place that customers look when they open or scan a menu.
3. It is best for a restaurant to remove unpopular but profitable menu items from the menu.
4. When designing a menu, it is standard to list the lowest priced items first and the most expensive items last.
5. "12 oz. prime rib" is an effective menu description.
6. Truth in menu laws require accuracy in describing food attributes, such as ingredients, preparation style, portion sizes, point of origin of the product, and health benefits.

Multiple Choice

1. A local steakhouse offers a dinner selection that consists of multiple courses including a starch, vegetable, and entrée. This type of menu is:
   a. à la carte.
   b. table d' hôte.
   c. cycle.
   d. all inclusive.
2. This type of menu allows customers to choose how much food they want to eat by pricing each item individually.
   a. À la carte menu
   b. Table d' hôte menu
   c. Cycle menu
   d. Mixed menu
3. Which is not an effective way to emphasize a menu item?
   a. Change the font size.
   b. Use different colors.
   c. Have pictures.
   d. Use a consistent font design.
4. This menu item should be the focal point of a menu or emphasized on a menu.
   a. Unpopular/unprofitable
   b. Unpopular/profitable
   c. Popular/unprofitable
   d. Popular/profitable
5. This refers to any product that is unique to an establishment, and cannot, or is not, recreated elsewhere.
   a. Popular dish
   b. Personal product
   c. Signature dish
   d. Focal point dish

Short Answer

1. What are the advantages and disadvantages of a table d' hôte menu compared to an à la carte menu?
2. Prepare a menu analysis using the following information:

Item	Sales	Food Cost	Selling Price
Item A	56	$7.95	$12.99
Item B	24	$8.29	$14.99
Item C	12	$5.90	$9.99
Item D	45	$4.33	$8.99
Item E	33	$4.25	$9.99

3. Describe the four main menu item categories and what management should do with the menu items in each category after conducting a menu analysis.
4. List four menu design principles that should be considered when creating a menu for a restaurant.

CHAPTER 14

True/False

1. Forecasting is important to control production, which will lead to the correct use of both labor and food supplies.
2. All forecasts are directly related to the historical data. For example, if a restaurant is forecasting for this coming summer, it is only necessary to review last summer's records.
3. If a server witnesses a customer pocketing silverware from the dining table, it is best that the server immediately confront the customer before he or she has a chance to leave the restaurant.
4. Theft is not uncommon in the hospitality industry. However, theft can be minimized if employers limit the number of people that handle cash.
5. Management's use of their knowledge and experience can play an important role in forecasting by helping to predict any variations in the numbers for the future, and make adjustments accordingly.

Multiple Choice

1. Weather conditions, the type of clients expected during the forecast period, and road conditions are examples of what type of data?
   a. Quantitative data
   b. Historical data
   c. Qualitative data
   d. Current data
2. This type of data includes previous sales separated by shift, product variety, day of the week, and other relevant factors.
   a. Quantitative data
   b. Historical data
   c. Qualitative data
   d. Both a and b
3. This technological equipment allows management to easily track historical data.
   a. Historical data file
   b. Point of sales system
   c. Production schedule
   d. Hand-held forecaster
4. All of the following are common ways to ensure that employees handling cash are responsible and reliable people in the hospitality industry, except:
   a. bonding of employees.
   b. background checks.
   c. reference checks.
   d. pre-employment screening tests.
5. A restaurant ensures that what is missing at the end of a shift was either sold or accounted for through other means by preparing a:
   a. total guest check report.
   b. POS system report.
   c. cashier's report.
   d. post-service sales checklist.

6. Which is a negative aspect of accepting credit cards as a form of payment in a restaurant?
   a. Increased sales from welcoming a larger clientele
   b. Company fees paid for the ability to accept credit cards
   c. Removing cash from servers' responsibility
   d. An additional credit card machine is needed.

Short Answer

1. What are the six steps to proper forecasting?
2. Describe the advantages of using a POS system in a restaurant.
3. If a restaurant forecasts 205 covers and usually sells 40% of their customers a dessert, how many of each item was sold using the following menu mix?

Chocolate soufflé:	21%
Apple blossom with ice cream:	33%
Raspberry cheesecake:	15%
Key lime pie:	12%
Cream puff sample:	19%

4. In question 3, if management wanted to increase dessert sales by 22%, how many new customers need to order a dessert?

CHAPTER 15

True/False

1. The first step to a successful business is understanding the customer.
2. The selling price first method is the most common method utilized to develop menu prices.
3. The main objective of correctly pricing menu items is to allow sales dollars to cover variable costs and create a contribution margin that will cover fixed costs and create profit.
4. The best method of suggestive selling is to promote the highest priced menu items.
5. A pre-shift meeting is when management comes together to discuss the successes and failures of the previous shift.
6. Employee empowerment is based on the principle that if employees feel they are needed by the organization as much as they need the organization, and the leaders understand that employees are the most valuable assets in the firm, then employees will work to their fullest ability.

Multiple Choice

1. If a restaurant has a signature dish on its menu, its menu price should be determined using which of the following methods?
   a. Selling price first
   b. Differentiated price
   c. Actual cost
   d. Contribution margin
2. This method of determining menu price requires the knowledge of projected costs of ingredients and a predetermined food cost percent.
   a. Selling price first
   b. Differentiated price
   c. Actual cost
   d. Contribution margin
3. A downside to offering early bird specials is:
   a. opening the restaurant early.
   b. having to create a new menu.
   c. taking away customers that would have come during normal hours.
   d. having to hire additional staff.
4. Which is not an example of suggestive selling?
   a. Would you like to start off with a drink?
   b. Would you like to supersize that?
   c. Would you like to try one of our desserts?
   d. Would you like some fresh cracked pepper on your salad?
5. All of the following should be discussed during a pre-shift meeting except:
   a. everyone's weekend plans.
   b. upcoming events, larger parties, and special guests.
   c. successful sales and up-selling techniques.
   d. specials and promotions.

Short Answer

1. Explain how a restaurant can diversify its clientele.
2. What is suggestive selling, and what are its advantages?
3. Why is employee empowerment an important part of the hospitality industry?
4. Calculate food cost and selling price per serving given the following information:

   Ingredient list/prices
   Romaine lettuce @ $0.89 per lb.
   Carrots @ $0.23 per lb.
   Eggs @ $1.19 per dozen
   Tomatoes @ $0.52 per lb.
   Croutons @ $0.99 per lb.
   Ranch dressing @ $4.00 per gal.

   Recipe: Salad (yields 12 servings)
   3 lb. romaine lettuce
   2 lb. carrots
   12 eggs
   1 lb. 4 oz. tomatoes
   6 oz. croutons
   2 qt. ranch dressing
   Food cost is 23%

Answers to Test Bank Questions

CHAPTER 1

True/False

1. True
2. True
3. False
4. True
5. False
6. False

Multiple Choice

1. c
2. a
3. d
4. c
5. b

Short Answer

1. Hamburger—16.81%
   Cheeseburger—29.22%
   Double cheeseburger—35.67%
   Chicken burger—12.55%
   Fish burger—5.74%
2. Any of the following are correct: Rent, insurance, salaried employees, taxes, depreciation
3. Food, beverage, non-salaried employees

CHAPTER 2

True/False

1. True
2. False
3. False
4. False
5. True
6. True

Multiple Choice

1. a
2. b
3. b
4. d
5. d

Short Answer

1. It is important to establish standards because without establishing policies and standards that are based on the expectations of the forecasted customer base, management cannot create the appropriate environment to maintain customer satisfaction and create repeat business.
2. Quality standard is the standard that an establishment has regarding the quality of its products. Quality standards should be established for food, tableware, equipment, décor, and other facets of the operation. Prime grade beef is a quality standard example of food, and silver flatware is a quality standard example of tableware.
3. Quantity standard is the standard that an establishment has regarding the quantity of food, labor, and supplies. Serving eight shrimp per serving of shrimp scampi is a quantity standard example of food, and having one waiter per table is a quantity standard example of labor.
4. Cost/price standard is the standard associated with the raw costs of items, as well as the menu price. The cost/price standard can be established by setting a predetermined food cost percent, and then calculating a menu price, setting a menu price that reflects the cost of raw goods, or setting a menu price based on its perceived value. An example of a cost/price standard is having a food cost percent of 27%.

5.

Sales	
Food	$945,032.40
Beverage	$171,067.57
Total Sales	$1,116,099.97
Cost of Sales	
Food	$255,158.75
Beverage	$25,660.14
Total Cost	$280,818.89
Gross Profit	$835,281.08
Controllable Expense	
Salaries	$89,288.00
Wages	$223,220.00
Employee benefits	$50,001.28
Other controllable expense	$66,966.00
Total controllable expense	$429,475.28
Gross Income	$405,805.80
Occupancy costs	$26,893.00
Interest	$7,341.00
Depreciation	$12,000.00
Profit/Loss	$359,571.80

CHAPTER 3

True/False

1. False
2. True
3. False
4. True

Multiple Choice

1. b
2. a
3. d
4. a
5. c
6. d
7. d
8. b

Short Answer

1. Sous vide is a food packaging technique that combines fresh ingredients into various dishes, and then vacuum-packs them into individual portions. It is then cooked under a vacuum and chilled.

   Modified atmosphere packaging (MAP) is a process where a combination of carbon dioxide, nitrogen, and oxygen replaces the ordinary air in the food package. MAP provides for a low-oxygen environment, where foodborne pathogens are unable to thrive and inhibits spoilage.

   Ultra-high temperature pasteurization is the third packaging technique. Food products are brought to over the boiling point of 250°F for only a fraction of a second, sterilizing the product.
2. The savings are two-fold. First, the addition of moisture during cooking lessens the amount that evaporates from the meat. Second, the machine can be programmed to do much of the monitoring that is needed while cooking.

CHAPTER 4

True/False

1. True
2. False
3. True
4. True
5. False
6. True
7. True

Multiple Choice

1. c
2. b
3. c
4. b
5. b
6. d
7. c
8. b
9. c

Short Answer

1. The break-even point can be changed by raising prices, lowering the quality of the product being served, or lowering the quantity standard for the product or service. Raising prices can affect the break-even point both positively and negatively. If the product continues to produce sales despite the price increase, then raising the prices will generate more revenue and perhaps more profit. However, if raising the price on a product discourages guests from purchasing the product, then the establishment will have lower sales. Lowering the quality and quantity standards of a product could also have both positive and negative effects. Lowering the quality and quantity standards of a product lead to a higher contribution margin by lowering variable costs, which is good for the establishment. However, lowering quality and quantity standards may cause customer dissatisfaction and ultimately lower sales by creating non-repeat business.
2.

Item	Number Sold	Selling Price	VC	VR	CM	CR	Total Sales	Total VC	Total CM
Cheese	45	$11.99	$3.00	.2502	$8.99	.7498	$539.55	$135.00	$404.55
Pepperoni	60	$14.99	$3.27	.2181	$11.72	.7819	$974.35	$212.55	$761.80
Hawaiian	23	$15.99	$3.75	.2345	$12.24	.7655	$367.77	$86.25	$281.52
Sausage	52	$14.99	$4.00	.2668	$10.99	.7332	$779.48	$208.00	$571.48
Chicken	65	$17.99	$4.25	.2362	$13.74	.7638	$1,169.35	$276.25	$893.10
Total	250						$3,830.50	$918.05	$2,912.45

Average check = $3,830.50 / 250 = $15.32
Average variable rate = $918.05 / $3,830.50 = .2397 = 23.97%
Average contribution margin = $2,912.45 / 250 = $11.65

CHAPTER 5

True/False

1. False
2. False
3. True
4. False
5. False

Multiple Choice

1. b
2. a
3. c
4. c
5. b
6. d
7. c
8. a
9. c

Short Answer

1. Open bid purchasing is when an establishment sends out its specifications, usually using a Steward's Market Quotation Sheet, to a variety of companies that supply the items needed. Any of the companies can then place a bid on the items and send it back to the buyer. After all the suppliers have sent in their bids, the buyer uses the Steward's Market Quotation Sheet to compare the prices from each supplier and choose which supplier to purchase from. Seal bid purchasing is different from open bid purchasing in that sealed bids are not to be seen by anyone else except the buyer. In seal bid purchasing, the establishment sends out its specifications to suppliers and then examines every bid sent back before making a decision on which supplier to purchase from.

CHAPTER 6

True/False

1. False
2. True
3. False
4. True
5. True
6. False

Multiple Choice

1. c
2. d
3. c
4. a
5. b
6. c

Short Answer

1. It is important to check for quality, quantity, and cost standards during receiving to ensure that the products being delivered are in fact the products that were ordered. The quality of the products being received should be inspected and compared to a copy of the specifications written for each product to ensure that the products meet company standards. The quantity of the products being received should be counted or measured and compared to a copy of the purchase order to ensure that the amount being received was the amount ordered. Lastly, the delivery invoice should be compared with the purchase order to ensure that the prices being charged are the same as the prices agreed upon when ordered. Inspecting deliveries is essential, and the only way to ensure that the products being delivered meet the quality, quantity, and cost standards of an establishment.
2.

Method	Ending Inventory Value	Cost of Food Issued
FIFO	$55.80	$216.04
LIFO	$53.50	$218.34
Actual	Cannot be determined	Cannot be determined
Latest Purchase Price	$59.00	$212.84
Weighted Price	$54.40	$217.44

3. Having a high inventory turnover means that the operation is spending extra money on the costs associated with purchasing. Also, if an establishment has a high inventory turnover, there is a potential of running out of an item, which can be risky. Having a low inventory turnover means that there is money tied up in inventory. Management should investigate and see where the establishment could be using its money more efficiently.

CHAPTER 7

True/False

1. True
2. True
3. False
4. False
5. True
6. False

Multiple Choice

1. c
2. d
3. b
4. b
5. a

Short Answer

1. Some of the causes and results of under production include pilferage, spoilage, inadequate portion size, and failure to follow a recipe. Pilferage and spoilage cause a decrease in production as a result of products being lost. If items are being stolen, systems need to be implemented to control inventory. Spoilage can be minimized by practicing FIFO. If a chef is preparing dishes that are larger than the planned portion size, this will result in under production. In this case, management should investigate and make changes to ensure that the correct portion sizes are being served. Finally, failure to follow a standardized recipe may yield less product than intended. If there is less yield, but the same portion sizes are being served, this will lead to under production. Management should either implement some controls to ensure that the kitchen staff is following the standardized recipe, or revise the standardized recipe.
2. The main factor that needs to be taken into consideration is the price of purchasing a large cut compared to the price of purchasing smaller ready-to-use-cuts. Other factors include whether or not the operation has the knowledge and skill to butcher the meat, there is a place to butcher it, and the by-products can be used.
3. The total cost approach takes the total cost for a product (tenderloin) and divides that by the number of main items (filets) prepared from it. All of the by-products (tips and ground beef) are considered free as far as food cost is concerned.
4.

Date	Food cost today	Food cost to date	Food cost % today	Food cost % to date	Food sales today	Food sales to date
2/5	$1,180	$1,180	34.48%	34.48%	$3,422	$3,422
2/6	$705	$1,885	16.36%	24.38%	$4,310	$7,732
2/7	$321	$2,206	8.65%	19.28%	$3,709	$11,441

5.

Butcher's Yield							
Item: Two ribs of beef Total Cost: $367.43			Grade: U.S. Choice Weight: 57 lb. 8 oz. AP Cost: $6.39/lb.				
	Weight		Ratio to Value			EP Cost	Multiplier
Breakdown	Lb.	Oz.	Total Lb.	Per Lb.	Total Value	Lb./Oz.	Lb./Oz.
Fat	8	6	14.57	$0.10	$0.84		
Bones	5	0	8.70	$0.45	$2.25		
Short ribs	4	4	7.39	$3.12	$13.26		
Ground beef	3	12	6.52	$1.19	$4.46		
Loss in cutting	0	6	0.65				
Prime rib	35	12	62.17		$346.62	$9.70	1.52
Total	57	8	100	$6.39	$367.43		

Cooking Loss							
	Weight		Ratio to Value			EP Cost	Multiplier
Breakdown	Lb.	Oz.	Total Lb.	Per Lb.	Total Value	Lb./Oz.	Lb./Oz.
Original weight	57	8	100	$6.39	$367.43		
Trimmed weight	35	12	62.17	$9.70	$346.62		
Loss in trimming	21	12	37.83				
Cooked weight	33	8	58.26				
Loss in cooking	2	4	3.91				
Bones and trim	2	0	3.48				
Saleable weight	31	8	54.78		$346.62	$11.00	1.72

6. a. Saleable weight = 31 lb. 8 oz.
   31.5 lbs × 16 oz. = 504 oz.
   504 oz. / 12 oz. = 42
   This product will yield 42 portions.

   b. 200 portions × 12 oz. = 2400 oz.
   2400 oz. / 16 oz. = 150 lbs.

$$\frac{54.78}{100} = \frac{150}{x}$$

   x = 273 lb. 13 oz. or 2400 / .5478 = 4381.16 / 16 = 273.82

   273 lb. 13 oz. of beef needs to be purchased.

   c. $11.00 × 12 oz. / 16 oz. = $8.25 (EP cost per serving)

   d. $6.73 × 1.72 = $11.58 (EP cost per lb.)
   $11.58 × 12 oz. / 16 oz. = $8.66 (new EP cost per serving)

CHAPTER 8

True/False

1. True
2. False
3. True
4. False
5. True
6. False
7. True

Multiple Choice

1. b
2. c
3. c
4. a
5. c

Short Answer

1. The advantages of a licensed state include credit availability, delivery, ability to negotiate prices, and competitive pricing. The disadvantages of a control state include no credit availability, delivery, or ability to negotiate prices, and less competitive pricing.
2. Canned and bottled beers are pasteurized, and can be stored at room temperature. However, the quality of beer will lessen over time. FIFO practices should be carried out when issuing canned and bottled beers, and they should be used within three months. Keg beer has not been pasteurized, so it should be stored in the refrigerator and used within one month. Proper wine storage varies depending on each particular bottle. All wines should be stored with 75 percent humidity. The storage temperature for wines depends on the wine being stored. Corked wines should be stored on an angle to allow the cork to stay moist. Screw-capped wines can be stored upright. Spirits are shelf stable and do not need to be refrigerated.
3. The two most common practices implemented when establishing issuing standards are control from misuse and cost accountability. To control misuse, management should limit the number of people allowed to requisition alcohol. It is best to allow only certain managers to requisition product from inventory, and only for the bar or outlet they supervise. To further control products from being misused, a list of products that each bar uses should be created to ensure that a bar not requisition unnecessary products. Cost accountability can easily be controlled through the usage of computerization. Some establishments require employees to turn in an empty bottle in exchange for a full bottle out of storage. This process is used to control issuance, and ensures that every bottle is accounted for. Other establishments implement a checkout system in which a person is in charge of checking all warehouse orders and confirming all deliveries.

CHAPTER 9

True/False

1. False
2. True
3. True
4. False
5. False
6. True
7. False

Multiple Choice

1. b
2. d
3. d
4. b
5. b
6. a

Short Answer

1. It is a good idea for management to develop standardized recipes for beverages because they serve as effective measuring controls. Using standardized recipes allows for a consistent product that will yield customer satisfaction, per-drink cost accountability, and purchasing and storage control.
2. The type of glassware used in an establishment is very important in beverage purchasing and production control because all glassware are different shapes and sizes. A bottle of wine would yield more glasses if smaller glasses were being used. For example, a half barrel of beer would yield 264 10 oz.-hour glasses with a 1″ head, but only 198 13 oz.-hour glasses with a 1″ head. Also, lined and unlined glasses can affect production control. A lined glass may appear to be full and actually contain less beverage than an unlined glass. Therefore, using glasses of various sizes and types within one operation may make the beverage purchasing process more difficult since there is less control over the distribution.
3. - Over-pouring drinks to get a larger tip
   - Under-pouring to build a bank of liquor to sell later and pocket the difference
   - Bringing in his or her own liquor and pocketing the sales
   - Offering complimentary drinks to get larger tips
   - Giving free drinks to friends
   - Ringing bottled beer as draft and pocketing the difference
   - Ringing a sales on the "no sale" key and pocketing the difference
   - Claiming someone walked out without paying, then pocketing the difference
   - Faking a broken bottle, and then pocketing the sales from selling the contents
   - Making a drink wrong, then selling it to someone else and pocketing the difference
   - Circumventing a pouring spout control system

CHAPTER 10

True/False

1. True
2. False
3. True
4. False
5. True

Multiple Choice

1. d
2. b
3. d
4. a
5. b
6. c

Short Answer

1. Salaried employees are considered fixed and non-controllable expenses, so the costs associated with them do not change with the change of sales. This means that salaried employees receive the same pay every period regardless of how many hours are worked. Hourly employees are considered variable and controllable expenses, so the costs associated with them will vary with the fluctuations in sales. Having hourly employees allows for flexibility in schedules during slow periods.
2. Improper training of employees is one of the biggest causes of turnover. If employees are not properly trained, their chances of a successful long-term employment are minimized. Also, if employees are improperly trained, it is difficult for employees to meet management's expectations because they are unaware of what is expected of them. Furthermore, improper training can lead to employee dissatisfaction due to the discrepancies between the employee's work and management's expectation.
3. One of the advantages of outsourcing is the ability to keep costs under control. Outsourcing allows an establishment to strengthen its employment capacity without increasing its personnel. Also, outsourcing provides access to experts with skills and expertise, while allowing organizations to focus on their core business objectives.
4. Any of the following are correct: Social Security, Medicare, unemployment, health insurance, dental, disability, paid holidays, educational assistance, concierge service, exercise facility, childcare, meals, flexible schedules, telecommuting, moving expenses, signing bonus, housing, low interest loans, golden parachutes.

CHAPTER 11

True/False

1. True
2. True
3. True
4. True
5. False
6. False
7. True

Multiple Choice

1. a
2. b
3. a
4. c
5. a

Short Answer

1. A job description is a detailed description of when and where specific tasks need to be performed. Having clearly defined job descriptions allows all employees to perform their jobs effectively and efficiently because they know what is expected of them.
2. • Management can work to get employees to "buy in" to the philosophy and goals of the company. If employees are working towards the company's goals, both the employee and management will be happy and successful.
   - Management can offer external rewards that can act as a motivational tool. If employees are working towards external rewards, they will be more likely to work harder towards achieving management's goals.
   - Management can acknowledge employees with internal rewards such as a compliment. These internal rewards will make employees feel appreciated and encourage them to continue doing their jobs well.
   - Management can create and maintain a positive work environment for its employees so that they will feel comfortable and satisfied with their job surroundings.
   - Employers should always keep staff informed about what is going on. With an open door policy, employees will feel comfortable communicating with employers and managers. This will allow employees to feel that they are wanted and needed as a part of the work process.
3. • Mystery shoppers are often used to monitor a company. The company hires and trains individuals to utilize the services of the company to monitor the success or failures of the operation. Mystery shoppers shop at the company and report back their findings. Using mystery shoppers is an excellent way to test one's own company and monitor its staff and services.
   - Guest satisfaction inquiries, indexes, and surveys are measuring tools used to collect information from customers regarding their overall satisfaction with the company. The

information collected is a way of monitoring the company and seeing what things are working for the company and other things that may need to be modified.

- The government health department is often used as a monitoring method in the restaurant industry. Health and safety standards are established by the local government, so publicized health reports or health ratings of a company are ways to keep the company in check.
- Rating systems such as the Mobil star and the AAA diamond ratings are monitoring methods that are very influential for both the company and its guests. These ratings are given on the basis of standards that an establishment has met. Therefore, if a company has a low rating, guests should be wary when visiting.

CHAPTER 12

True/False

1. True
2. False
3. True

Multiple Choice

1. b
2. d
3. d

Short Answer

1. Franchise fees are a percentage of sales that franchisees must pay to the franchisor in exchange for the right to sell their product.
2. - Purchase reconditioned or rebuilt equipment.
   - Obtain used equipment through auctions.
   - Purchase demonstration equipment.
   - Purchase directly from the manufacturer, bypassing the distributor or retailer.
3. - Land and building ownership is the largest expense. There are many options for the facility depending on the location and the type of operation. Land and building can be purchased and owned, or can be leased.
   - If a company decides to lease property, it must pay rent, usually a fixed monthly fee for an agreed upon length of time.
   - Insurance expenses are costs associated with occupancies of many businesses. Some business insurances are optional while others are required by law. These include worker's compensation, property, and liability insurance.
   - The landscape of a building is another expense associated with occupancy. If grass is part of the landscape design, expenses such as watering and maintaining the grass need to be taken into consideration.
   - There are many expenses that are associated with the upkeep of an establishment's parking lot. Some expenses may include snow removal, repaving, repainting of lines, lighting, security, and valet services. The parking lot is the first and last impression of a guest's experience, so it is important for a restaurant or hotel to maintain it.

- Building maintenance is important and may include costs such as window cleaning, snow removal, sign maintenance, and keeping the building safe, up-to-date, and working properly. These expenses can be costly and many are mandated by city building codes and health department regulations. Additional building maintenance expenses can include maintenance or replacement of heating and air conditioning units, fixing leaking ceilings, and maintaining proper plumbing to meet city, state, and health department criteria.
- The hospitality industry needs to pay local, state, and federal taxes based on the rates established in the community and the volume of business and profit generated.

CHAPTER 13

True/False

1. False
2. True
3. False
4. False
5. False
6. True

Multiple Choice

1. b
2. a
3. d
4. b
5. c

Short Answer

1.

Advantages of a table d' hôte menu	Advantages of an à la carte menu
Price changes are easy	Possible check average increase
Increased turnover	Customer choice
Limited variety in the kitchen	
Disadvantages of a table d' hôte menu	**Disadvantages of an à la carte menu**
Possible food waste	Extra purchasing and preparation
Higher menu price	Added controls needed
Guest feels less in charge	

2.

Item	Sales	Menu Mix	Food Cost	Selling Price	CM	Total Costs	Total Revenue	Total CM
Item A	**56**	32.94%	**$7.95**	**$12.99**	$5.04	$445.20	$727.44	$282.24
Item B	**24**	14.12%	**$8.29**	**$14.99**	$6.70	$198.96	$359.76	$160.80
Item C	**12**	7.06%	**$5.90**	**$9.99**	$4.09	$70.80	$119.88	$49.08
Item D	**45**	26.47%	**$4.33**	**$8.99**	$4.66	$194.85	$404.55	$209.70
Item E	**33**	19.41%	**$4.25**	**$9.99**	$5.74	$140.25	$329.67	$189.42
Total	170	100.00%				$1,050.06	$1,941.30	$891.24

Average Contribution Margin: $26.23 / 5 = $5.25
Popularity Index: 1 / 5 × 0.7 = 14.0%
Food Cost %: $1,050.06 / $1,941.30 = 54.09%

Item A: Popular/unprofitable
Item B: Popular/profitable
Item C: Unpopular/unprofitable
Item D: Popular/unprofitable
Item E: Popular/profitable

3.
- Unpopular/unprofitable menu items are those that are not sold frequently, and when they do sell, they do not generate a profit. Sometimes management decides that unpopular/unprofitable items should be left on the menu either because they are a staple of the menu, or because there are a few customers who like them. However, these items should be removed from the menu because they are not helping the contribution margin.
- Unpopular/profitable menu items are those that do not sell well, but generate a large contribution margin when they do sell. These are the items that should be marketed better. Such marketing strategies include advertisement, samples to guests, and promoting the items through specials. Unpopular/profitable items should be the focal point of the menu or emphasized on the menu or through suggestive selling.

- Popular/unprofitable menu items are customer favorites that do not generate a large contribution margin. These items need be re-evaluated and management should implement a change in the quality, quantity, or cost standard associated with the dish. The quality or quantity standard of the dish will have to be lowered, or the menu cost will need to be raised. However, if customers are not satisfied with the change in quality, quantity, or cost, then management should think about removing the item from the menu.
- Popular/profitable menu items are dishes that include a restaurant's signature dishes. These items should be left alone, as they are doing what they should be doing.

4. - Unpopular/profitable items should be the focal point of a menu.
   - Do not list menu items according to price.
   - If a menu category starts on one page, it should finish on the same page, not separated onto two pages.
   - The physical menu design (quality of paper, binding, font, color, size, and illustrations) should reflect the quality and type of the restaurant.
   - It is important to have menu diversity. Offer a wide array of items to attract a variety of customers without being too diverse, overwhelming the kitchen.
   - Menu items should ideally include different products that allow for total utilization of raw products.
   - Use effective menu descriptions. Sentences should be short, concise, and include eye-catching words.
   - Adhere to truth in advertising. Use accurate information when describing menu items.

CHAPTER 14

True/False

1. True
2. False
3. False
4. True
5. True

Multiple Choice

1. c
2. d
3. b
4. a
5. d
6. b

Short Answer

1. 1. Predict the number of customers (covers, historical quantitative data).
   2. Check surroundings (qualitative data).
   3. Establish total expected sales (current data).
   4. Use popularity index (menu mix).
   5. Prepare a production schedule.
   6. Monitor/reconcile and correct for the future (re-evaluate for future use).
2. A POS system is essential in a restaurant. Servers can ring up orders on the system, which will print up in the area that is going to prepare the food or beverage. It ensures that no food leaves the kitchen without a computer-generated order coming in. Also, a POS system minimizes conversation between the front-of-the-house and the back-of-the-house. Another advantage is that in most cases, only management can delete something off a bill, lowering the chance for sales to go unreported. A POS system acts as a major control system in a restaurant.
3. $205 \times 0.40 = 82$ customers

   Chocolate soufflé: $82 \times 0.21 = 17$

   Apple blossom: $82 \times 0.33 = 27$

   Raspberry cheesecake: $82 \times 0.15 = 12$

   Key lime pie: $82 \times 0.12 = 10$

   Cream puff sample: $82 \times 0.19 = 16$
4. $82 \times 1.22 = 100$ customers

   $100 / x = 0.40 / 1.00$

   $x = 250$

   $250 - 205 = 45$ new customers

CHAPTER 15

True/False

1. True
2. False
3. True
4. False
5. False
6. True

Multiple Choice

1. b
2. c
3. c
4. d
5. a

Short Answer

1. A restaurant can diversify its clientele by offering a special that targets a different audience than the owner originally had envisioned. For example, a restaurant can open up its doors earlier and offer an early bird special. This will bring in new customers that would otherwise not have eaten at the restaurant during normal hours at normal prices. Another way to attract new customers is to open up as a night club during the evening when the restaurant would normally be closed. A night club targets a whole new audience than that of a restaurant. By opening its doors during normally closed hours, a restaurant can increase its sales and market to a different audience. Early bird specials or a night club may even attract and influence guests to return during the normal working hours of the restaurant.
2. Suggestive selling is used by employees to increase check averages, profit margin, and customer satisfaction. If suggestive selling is implemented correctly, it can create a win–win situation for the guest, the server, and the owner. One method of suggestive selling is to sell an additional course, such as an appetizer or a dessert. Another method of suggestive selling is to promote a menu item that has a higher contribution margin. Suggestive selling is simple and can be done by simply asking a customer a question such as, "Would you like fries with that?" Suggestive selling is effective and provides satisfaction for all. The owner or manager will be satisfied with increased sales and increased profits. The customer will have had a fulfilling dining experience and memorable meal. The server will have enhanced the customer's experience and received an increase in tips.
3. Employee empowerment gives the employees resources to placate a dissatisfied customer immediately. Employees already have direct contact and interaction with the customers, and if they have the ability to solve guests' problems quickly and efficiently, the level of customer service and customer satisfaction will increase. This gives employees the authority to make a customer's dining experience as positive as possible without having to complicate things with management. Employee empowerment will make guests feel better, and in return, guests are likely to share their experience with others using positive word-of-mouth.
4. **Recipe: Salad (yields 12 servings)**

   3 lb. romaine lettuce
   2 lb. carrots
   12 eggs
   1 lb. 4 oz. tomatoes
   6 oz. croutons
   2 qt. ranch dressing

   Food cost is 23%

   Romaine: 3 × 0.89 = $2.67
   Carrots: 2 × 0.23 = $0.46
   Eggs: 1 × 1.19 = $1.19
   Tomatoes: 1.25 × 0.52 = $0.65
   Croutons: 0.375 × 0.99 = $0.37
   Ranch: 0.5 × 4.00 = $2.00
   Total cost = $7.34
   Food cost: 7.34 / 12 = $0.61 per serving
   Selling Price: 0.61 / 0.23 = $2.65 per serving